ARCHITECT REGISTRATION EXAM

BUILDING SYSTEMS

ARE SAMPLE PROBLEMS AND PRACTICE EXAM

SECOND EDITION

HOLLY WILLIAMS LEPPO, RA/CID
DAVID KENT BALLAST, FAIA

The Power to Pass®
www.ppi2pass.com

Professional Publications, Inc. • Belmont, California

Benefit by Registering This Book with PPI

- Get book updates and corrections.
- Hear the latest exam news.
- Obtain exclusive exam tips and strategies.
- Receive special discounts.

Register your book at **www.ppi2pass.com/register**.

Report Errors and View Corrections for This Book

PPI is grateful to every reader who notifies us of a possible error. Your feedback allows us to improve the quality and accuracy of our products. You can report errata and view corrections at **www.ppi2pass.com/errata**.

LEED® and USGBC® are registered trademarks of the U.S. Green Building Council.

National Electrical Code®, NEC®, and NFPA® are registered trademarks of the National Fire Protection Association.

MasterSpec® is a registered trademark of ARCOM.

BUILDING SYSTEMS: ARE SAMPLE PROBLEMS AND PRACTICE EXAM
Second Edition

Current printing of this edition: 1

Printing History

edition number	printing number	update
1	3	Minor corrections. Vignette update.
1	4	Minor corrections. Copyright update.
2	1	New edition. Code update. Copyright update.

Printed in the United States of America.

PPI
1250 Fifth Avenue, Belmont, CA 94002
(650) 593-9119
www.ppi2pass.com

ISBN: 978-1-59126-329-6

Library of Congress Control Number: 2010941642

TABLE OF CONTENTS

Preface and Acknowledgments v

Introduction vii

How to Use This Book xv

How SI Units Are Used in This Book xvii

Codes and Standards Used in This Book xix

Recommended Reading xxi

Sample Problems
    Codes and Regulations 1
    Environmental Issues 4
    Plumbing 10
    HVAC 15
    Electrical 21
    Lighting 24
    Acoustics 28
    Specialties 32
    Mechanical and Electrical Plan Vignette 35

Practice Exam: Multiple Choice 43

Practice Exam: Vignette
    Mechanical and Electrical Plan 59

Practice Exam: Multiple Choice Solutions 63

Practice Exam: Vignette Solution
    Mechanical and Electrical Plan 83

PREFACE AND ACKNOWLEDGMENTS

This book is tailored to the needs of those studying for the Architect Registration Examination (ARE). For the second edition, we have updated the content to reflect the July 2010 update of the *ARE 4.0 Guidelines*, as well as the most recent editions of a number of codes and standards, including

- 2005 *Americans with Disabilities Act and Architectural Barriers Act Accessibility Guidelines*
- 2008 ACI 318 *Building Code Requirements for Structural Concrete*
- 2009 *International Building Code*
- 2010 CSI MasterFormat

In the ARE, there is considerable overlap in what you need to study for the various divisions. For this reason, the *ARE Review Manual* covers all the divisions of the ARE in a single volume. This book, *Building Systems: ARE Sample Problems and Practice Exam*, is one of seven companion volumes, one for each ARE division. We believe that this organization will help you study for individual divisions most effectively.

You will find that this book and the related volumes are valuable parts of your exam preparation. Although there is no substitute for a good formal education and the broad-based experience provided by your internship with a practicing architect, this review series will help you direct your study efforts to increase your chances of passing the ARE.

Many people have helped in the production of this book. We would like to thank all the fine people at PPI including Scott Marley (project editor), Cathy Schrott (typesetter), Amy Schwertman (cover designer and illustrator), and Thomas Bergstrom (illustrator).

Although we had much help in preparing this new edition, the responsibility for any errors is our own. A current list of known errata for this book is maintained at **www.ppi2pass.com/errata**, and you can let us know of any errors you find at the same place. We greatly appreciate the time our readers take to help us keep this book accurate and up to date.

Holly Williams Leppo, RA/CID
David Kent Ballast, FAIA

INTRODUCTION

ABOUT THIS BOOK

Building Systems: ARE Sample Problems and Practice Exam is written to help you prepare for the Building Systems division of the Architect Registration Examination (ARE).

Although this book can be a valuable study aid by itself, it is designed to be used along with the *ARE Review Manual*, also published by PPI. The *ARE Review Manual* is organized into sections that cover all seven divisions of the ARE.

- Programming, Planning & Practice
- Site Planning & Design
- Schematic Design
- Structural Systems
- Building Systems
- Building Design & Construction Systems
- Construction Documents & Services

This book is one of seven companion volumes to the *ARE Review Manual* that PPI publishes. Each of these books contains sample problems and practice exams for one of the ARE divisions.

- *Programming, Planning & Practice: ARE Sample Problems and Practice Exam*
- *Site Planning & Design: ARE Sample Problems and Practice Exam*
- *Schematic Design: ARE Sample Problems and Practice Exam*
- *Structural Systems: ARE Sample Problems and Practice Exam*
- *Building Systems: ARE Sample Problems and Practice Exam*
- *Building Design & Construction Systems: ARE Sample Problems and Practice Exam*
- *Construction Documents & Services: ARE Sample Problems and Practice Exam*

THE ARCHITECT REGISTRATION EXAMINATION

Congratulations on completing (or nearing the end of) the Intern Development Program! You are two-thirds of the way to being able to call yourself an architect. NAAB degree? Check. IDP? Check. Now on to step three.

The final hurdle is the Architect Registration Examination. The ARE is a uniform test administered to candidates who wish to become licensed architects after they have served their required internships. It is given throughout the United States, the U.S. territories, and Canada.

The ARE has been developed to protect the health, safety, and welfare of the public by testing a candidate's entry-level competence to practice architecture. Its content relates as closely as possible to situations encountered in practice. It tests for the kinds of knowledge, skills, and abilities required of an entry-level architect, with particular emphasis on those services that affect public health, safety, and welfare. In order to accomplish these objectives, the exam tests for

- knowledge in specific subject areas
- the ability to make decisions
- the ability to consolidate and use information to solve a problem
- the ability to coordinate the activities of others on the building team

The ARE also includes some professional practice and project management problems, and problems that are based on particular editions of codes as specified in the *ARE 4.0 Guidelines*. (However, the editions specified by the *ARE Guidelines* are not necessarily the most current editions available.)

The ARE is developed jointly by the National Council of Architectural Registration Boards (NCARB) and the Committee of Canadian Architectural Councils (CCAC), with the assistance of the Chauncey Group International and

Prometric. The Chauncey Group serves as NCARB's test development and operations consultant, and Prometric operates and maintains the test centers where the ARE is administered.

Although the responsibility of professional licensing rests with each individual state, every state's board requires successful completion of the ARE to achieve registration or licensure. One of the primary reasons for a uniform test is to facilitate reciprocity—that is, to enable an architect to more easily gain a license to practice in states other than the one in which he or she was originally licensed.

The ARE is administered and graded entirely by computer. All divisions of the exam are offered six days a week at a network of test centers across North America. The results are scored by computer, and the results are forwarded to individual state boards of architecture, which process them and send them to candidates. If you fail a division, you must wait six months before you can retake that division.

First Steps

As you begin to prepare for the exam, you should first obtain a current copy of the *ARE Guidelines* from NCARB. This booklet will get you started with the exam process and will be a valuable reference throughout. It includes descriptions of the seven divisions, instructions on how to apply, pay for, and take the ARE, and other useful information. You can download a PDF version at www.ncarb.org, or you can request a printed copy through the contact information provided at that site.

The NCARB website also gives current information about the exam, education requirements, training, examination procedures, and NCARB reciprocity services. It includes sample scenarios of the computer-based examination process and examples of costs associated with taking the computer-based exam.

The PPI website is also a good source of exam info (at **www.ppi2pass.com/areinfo**) and answers to frequently asked questions (at **www.ppi2pass.com/arefaq**).

To register as an examinee, you should obtain the registration requirements from the board in the state, province, or territory where you want to be registered. The exact requirements vary from one jurisdiction to another, so contact your local board. Links to state boards can be found at **www.ppi2pass.com/areinfo**.

As soon as NCARB has verified your qualifications and you have received your "Authorization to Test" letter, you may begin scheduling examinations. The exams are offered on a first come, first served basis and must be scheduled at least 72 hours in advance. See the *ARE Guidelines* for instructions on finding a current list of testing centers. You may take the exams at any location, even outside the state in which you intend to become registered.

You may schedule any division of the ARE at any time and may take the divisions in any order. Divisions can be taken one at a time, to spread out preparation time and exam costs, or can be taken together in any combination.

However, you must pass all seven divisions of the ARE within a single five-year period. This period, or "rolling clock," begins on the date of the first division you passed. If you have not completed the ARE within five years, the divisions that you passed more than five years ago are no longer credited, and the content in them must be retaken. Your new five-year period begins on the date of the earliest division you passed within the last five years.

Examination Format

The ARE is organized into seven divisions that test various areas of architectural knowledge and problem-solving ability.

Programming, Planning & Practice

> 85 multiple-choice problems
> 1 graphic vignette: Site Zoning

Site Planning & Design

> 65 multiple-choice problems
> 2 graphic vignettes: Site Design, Site Grading

Schematic Design

> 2 graphic vignettes: Building Layout, Interior Layout

Structural Systems

> 125 multiple-choice problems
> 1 graphic vignette: Structural Layout

Building Systems

> 95 multiple-choice problems
> 1 graphic vignette: Mechanical & Electrical Plan

Building Design & Construction Systems

> 85 multiple-choice problems
> 3 graphic vignettes: Accessibility/Ramp, Roof Plan, Stair Design

Construction Documents & Services

> 100 multiple-choice problems
> 1 graphic vignette: Building Section

Experienced test-takers will tell you that there is quite a bit of overlap among these divisions. Problems that seem better suited to the Construction Documents & Services division may show up on the Building Design & Construction Systems division, for example, and problems on architectural history and building regulations might show up anywhere. That's why it's important to have a comprehensive strategy for studying and taking the exams.

The ARE is given entirely by computer. There are two kinds of problems on the exam. Multiple-choice problems are short questions presented on the computer screen; you answer them by clicking on the right answer or answers, or by filling in a blank. Graphic vignettes are longer problems in design; you solve a vignette by planning and drawing your solution on the computer. Six of the seven divisions contain both multiple-choice sections and graphic vignettes; the Schematic Design division contains only vignettes. Both kinds of problems are described later in this Introduction.

STUDY GUIDELINES

After the five to seven years (or even more) of higher education you've received to this point, you probably have a good idea of the study strategy that works best for you. The trick is figuring out how to apply that to the ARE. Unlike many college courses, there isn't a textbook or set of class notes from which all the exam problems will be derived. The exams are very broad and draw problems from multiple areas of knowledge.

The first challenge, then, is figuring out what to study. The ARE is never quite the same exam twice. The field of knowledge tested is always the same, but the specific problems asked are drawn randomly from a large pool, and will differ from one candidate to the next. One division may contain many code-related problems for one candidate and only a few for the next. This makes the ARE a challenge to study for.

The *ARE Guidelines* contain lists of resources recommended by NCARB. That list can seem overwhelming, though, and on top of that, many of the recommended books are expensive or no longer in print. To help address this problem, PPI has published the *ARE Review Manual*, which gives you an overview of the concepts and information that will be most useful in passing the ARE. A list of helpful resources for preparing for the Building Systems division can also be found in the Recommended Reading section of this book.

Your method of studying for the ARE should be based on both the content and form of the exam and on your school and work experience. Because the exam covers such a broad range of subject matter, it cannot possibly include every detail of practice. Rather, it tends to focus on what is considered entry-level knowledge and knowledge that is important for the protection of the public's health, safety, and welfare. Other types of problems are asked, too, but this knowledge should be the focus of your review schedule.

Your recent work experience should also help you determine what areas to study the most. If, for example, you have been working with construction documents for several years, you will probably need less review in that area than in others you have not had much recent experience with.

The *ARE Review Manual* and its companion volumes are structured to help you focus on the topics that are more likely to be included in the exam in one form or another. Some subjects may seem familiar or may be easy to recall from memory, and others may seem completely foreign; the latter are the ones to give particular attention to. It may be wise to study additional sources on these subjects, take review seminars, or get special help from someone who is knowledgeable in the topic.

A typical candidate might spend about forty hours preparing for and taking each exam. Some will need to study more, some less. Forty hours is about one week of studying eight hours a day, or two weeks of four hours a day, or a month of two hours a day, along with reasonable breaks and time to attend to other responsibilities. As you probably work full time and have other family and personal obligations, it is important to develop a realistic schedule and do your best to stick to it. The ARE is not the kind of exam you can cram for the night before.

Also, since the fees are high and retaking a test is expensive, you want to do your best and pass in as few tries as possible. Allowing enough time to study and going into each exam well prepared will help you relax and concentrate on the problems.

The following steps may provide a useful structure for an exam study program.

Step 1: Start early. You can't review for a test like this by starting two weeks before the date. This is especially true if you are taking all portions of the exam for the first time.

Step 2: Go through the *ARE Review Manual* quickly to get a feeling for the scope of the subject matter and how the major topics are organized. Whatever division you're studying for, plan to review the chapters on building regulations as well. Review the *ARE Guidelines*.

Step 3: Based on your review of the *ARE Review Manual* and *ARE Guidelines*, and on a realistic appraisal of your strong and weak areas, set priorities for study and determine which topics need more study time.

Step 4: Divide review subjects into manageable units and organize them into a sequence of study. It is generally best to start with the less familiar subjects. Based on the exam date and plans for beginning study, assign a time limit to each study unit. Again, your knowledge of a subject should determine the time devoted to it. You may want to devote an entire week to earthquake design if it is an unfamiliar subject, and only one day to timber design if it is a familiar one. In setting up a schedule, be realistic about other life commitments as well as your personal ability to concentrate on studying over a length of time.

Step 5: Begin studying, and stick with the schedule. Of course, this is the most difficult part of the process and the one that requires the most self-discipline. The job should be easier if you have started early and if you are following a realistic schedule that allows time for recreation and personal commitments.

Step 6: Stop studying a day or two before the exam. Relax. By this time, no amount of additional cramming will help.

At some point in your studying, you will want to spend some time becoming familiar with the program you will be using to solve the graphic vignettes, which does not resemble commercial CAD software. The software and sample vignettes can be downloaded from the NCARB website at www.ncarb.org.

There are many schools of thought on the best order for taking the divisions. One factor to consider is the six-month waiting period before you can retake a particular division. It's never fun to predict what you might fail, but if you know that a specific area might give you trouble, consider taking that exam near the beginning. You might be pleasantly surprised when you check the mailbox, but if not, as you work through the rest of the exams, the clock will be ticking and you can schedule the retest six months later.

Here are some additional tips.

- Learn concepts first, and then details later. For example, it is much better to understand the basic ideas and theories of waterproofing than it is to attempt to memorize dozens of waterproofing products and details. Once the concept is clear, the details are much easier to learn and to apply during the exam.

- Use the *ARE Review Manual's* index to focus on particular subjects in which you feel weak, especially subjects that can apply to more than one division.

- Don't tackle all your hardest subjects first. Make one of your early exams one that you feel fairly confident about. It's nice to get off on the right foot with a PASS.

- Programming, Planning & Practice and Building Design & Construction Systems both tend to be "catch-all" divisions that cover a lot of material from the Construction Documents & Services division as well as others. Consider taking Construction Documents & Services first among those three, and then the other two soon after.

- Many past candidates recommend taking the Programming, Planning & Practice division last or nearly last, so that you will be familiar with the body of knowledge for all the other divisions as well.

- Brush up on architectural history before taking any of the divisions with multiple-choice sections. Know major buildings and their architects, particularly structures that are representative of an architect's philosophy (for example, Le Corbusier and the Villa Savoye) or that represent "firsts" or "turning points."

- Try to schedule your exams so that you'll have enough time to get yourself ready, eat, and review a little. If you'll have a long drive to the testing center, try to avoid having to make it during rush hour.

- If you are planning to take more than one division at a time, do not overstudy any one portion of the exam. It is generally better to review the concepts than to try to become an overnight expert in one area. For example, you may need to know general facts about plate girders, but you will not need to know how to complete a detailed design of a plate girder.

- Even though you may have a good grasp of the information and knowledge in a particular subject area, be prepared to address problems on the material in a variety of forms and from different points of view. For example, you may have studied and know definitions, but you will also need to be able to apply that knowledge when a problem includes a definition-type word as part of a more complex situation-type of problem.

- Solve as many sample problems as possible, including those provided with NCARB's practice program, the books of sample problems and practice exams published by PPI, and any others that are available.

- Take advantage of the community of intern architects going through this experience with you. Some local AIA chapters offer ARE preparation courses or may be able to help you organize a study group with other interns in your area. PPI's Passing Zones are interactive online reviews to help you prepare for individual divisions of the ARE. Find out more at **www.ppi2pass.com/passingzone**.

Visit website forums to discuss the exam with others who have taken it or are preparing to take it. The Architecture Exam Forum at **www.ppi2pass.com/ areforum** is a great online resource for questions, study advice, and encouragement. Even though the special problems on the ARE change daily, it is a good idea to get a feeling for the ARE's format, its general emphasis, and the subject areas that previous candidates have found particularly troublesome.

- A day or two before the first test session, stop studying in order to relax as much as possible. Get plenty of sleep the night before the test.

- Try to relax as much as possible during study periods and during the exam itself. Worrying is counterproductive. Candidates who have worked diligently in school, have obtained a wide range of experience during internship, and have started exam review early will be in the best possible position to pass the ARE.

TAKING THE EXAM

What to Bring

Bring multiple forms of photo ID and your Authorization to Test letter to the test site.

It is neither necessary nor permitted to bring any reference materials or scratch paper into the test site. Pencils and scratch paper are provided by the proctor and must be returned when leaving the exam room. Earplugs will also be provided. Leave all your books and notes in the car. Most testing centers have lockers for your keys, small personal belongings, and cell phone.

Do not bring a calculator into the test site. A calculator built into the testing software will be available in all divisions.

Arriving at the Testing Center

Allow plenty of time to get to the exam site, to avoid transportation problems such as getting lost or stuck in traffic jams. If you can, arrive a little early, and take a little time in the parking lot to review one last time the formulas and other things you need to memorize. Then relax, take a few deep breaths, and go take the exam.

Once at the test site, you will check in with the attendant, who will verify your identification and your Authorization to Test. (Don't forget to take this home with you after each exam; you'll need it for the next one.) After you check in, you'll be shown to your testing station.

When the exam begins, you will have the opportunity to click through a tutorial that explains how the computer program works. You'll probably want to read through it the first time, but after that initial exam, you will know how the software works and you won't need the tutorial. Take a deep breath, organize your paper and pencils, and take advantage of the opportunity to dump all the facts floating around in your brain onto your scratch paper—write down as much as you can.

This includes formulas, ratios ("if x increases, y decreases"), and so on—anything that you are trying desperately not to forget. If you can get all the things you've crammed at the last minute onto that paper, you'll be able to think a little more clearly about the problems posed on the screen.

Taking the Multiple-Choice Sections

The ARE multiple-choice sections include several types of problems.

One type of multiple-choice problem is based on written, graphic, or photographic information. You will need to examine the information and select the correct answer from four given options. Some problems may require calculations.

A second type of multiple-choice problem lists four or five items or statements, which are given Roman numerals from I to IV or I to V. For example, the problem may give five statements about a subject, and you must choose the statements that are true. The four answer choices are combinations of these numerals, such as "I and III" or "II, IV, and V."

A third type of multiple-choice problem describes a situation that could be encountered in actual practice. Drawings, diagrams, photographs, forms, tables, or other data may also be given. The problem requires you to select the best answer from four options.

Two kinds of problems that NCARB calls "alternate item types" also show up in the multiple-choice sections. In a "fill in the blank" problem, you must fill a blank with a number derived from a table or calculation. In a "check all that apply" problem, six options are given, and you must choose all the correct answers. The problem tells how many of the options are correct, from two to four. You must choose all the correct answers to receive credit; partial credit is not given.

Between 10% and 15% of the problems in a multiple-choice section will be these "alternate item type" problems. Every problem on the ARE, however, counts the same toward your total score.

Keep in mind that multiple-choice problems often require the examinee to do more than just select an answer based on memory. At times it will be necessary to combine several facts, analyze data, perform a calculation, or review a drawing. You will probably not need the entire time allotted for the multiple-choice sections. If you have time for more than one pass through the problems, you can make good use of it.

Here are some tips for the multiple-choice problems.

- Go through the entire section in one somewhat swift pass, answering the problems that you're sure about and marking the others so you can return to them later. If a problem requires calculations, skip it for now unless it's very simple. Then go back to the beginning and work your way through the exam again, taking a little more time to read each problem and think through the answer.

- Another benefit of going through the entire section at the beginning is that occasionally there is information in one problem that may help you answer another problem somewhere else.

- If you are very unsure of a problem, pick your best answer, mark it, and move on. You will probably have time at the end of the test to go back and recheck these answers. But remember, your first response is usually the best.

- Always answer all the problems. Unanswered problems are counted wrong, so even if you are just guessing, it's better to choose an answer and have a chance of it being correct than to skip it and be certain of getting it wrong. When faced with four options, the old SAT strategy of eliminating the two options that are definitely wrong and making your best guess between the two that remain is helpful on the ARE, too.

- Some problems may seem too simple. Although a few very easy and obvious problems are included on the ARE, more often the simplicity should serve as a red flag to warn you to reevaluate the problem for exceptions to a rule or special circumstances that make the obvious, easy response incorrect.

- Watch out for absolute words in a problem, such as "always," "never," and "completely." These are often a clue that some little exception exists, turning what reads like a true statement into a false one or vice versa.

- Be alert for words like "seldom," "usually," "best," and "most reasonable." These indicate that some judgment will be involved in answering the problem. Look for two or more options that appear to be very similar.

- Some divisions will provide an on-screen reference sheet with useful formulas and other information that will help you solve some problems. Skim through the reference sheet so you know what information is there, and then use it as a resource.

- Occasionally there may be a defective problem. This does not happen very often, but if it does, make the best choice possible under the circumstances. Flawed problems are usually discovered, and either they are not counted on the test or any one of the correct answers is credited.

Solving the Vignettes

Each of the eleven graphic vignettes on the ARE is designed to test a particular area of knowledge and skill. Each one presents a base plan of some kind and gives programmatic and other requirements. You must create a plan that satisfies the requirements. There is one Building Systems vignette.

For the *Mechanical and Electrical Plan vignette*, you are given a background drawing, a program, code requirements, and a lighting diagram, and must complete a reflected ceiling plan by placing the ceiling grid and arranging the mechanical and electrical system components within it. The problem can include considerations for structural element sizes, duct sizes and types, footcandle levels, fire dampers, rated vertical shafts, placement of diffusers, and mechanical system requirements.

The computer scores the vignettes by a complex grading method. Design criteria are given various point values, and responses are categorized as Acceptable, Unacceptable, or Indeterminate.

General Tips for the Vignettes

Here are some general tips for approaching the vignettes. More detailed solving tips can be found in the vignette solutions in this book.

- Remember that with the current format and computer grading, each vignette covers only a very specific area of knowledge and offers a limited number of possible solutions. In a few cases only one solution is really possible. Use this as an advantage.

- Read everything thoroughly, twice. Follow the requirements exactly, letting each problem solve itself as much as possible. Be careful not to read more into the instructions than is there. The test writers are very specific about what they want; there is no need to add to the vignette requirements. If a particular type of solution is strongly suggested, follow that lead.

- Consider only those code requirements given in the vignette, even if they deviate from familiar codes. Do not read anything more into the vignette. The code requirements may be slightly different from what you use in practice.

- Use the scratch paper provided to sketch possible solutions before starting the final solution.

- Make sure all programmed elements are included in the final design.

- When the functional requirements of the vignette have been solved, use the vignette directions as a checklist to make sure all criteria have been satisfied.

General Tips for Using the Vignette Software

It is important to practice with the vignette software that will be used in the exam. The program is unique to the ARE and unlike standard CAD software. If you are unfamiliar with the software interface you will waste valuable time learning to use it, and are likely to run out of time before completing the vignettes. Practice software can be downloaded at no charge from NCARB's website at www.ncarb.org. Usage time for the practice program can also be purchased at Prometric test centers. The practice software includes tutorials, directions, and one practice vignette for each of the eleven vignettes.

Here are some general tips for using the vignette software.

- When elements overlap on the screen, it may be difficult to select a particular element. If this happens, repeatedly click on the element without moving the mouse until the desired element is highlighted.

- Try to stay in "ortho" mode. This mode can be used to solve most vignettes, and it makes the solution process much easier and quicker. Unless obviously required by the vignette, creating additional angles only complicates things and eats up your limited time.

- If the vignette relates to contour modifications, it may help to draw schematic sections through the significant existing slopes. This provides a three-dimensional image of the situation.

- When drawing, if the program states that elements should connect, make sure they touch at their boundaries only and do not overlap. Use the *check* tool to determine if there are any overlaps. Walls that do not align correctly can cause a solution to be downgraded or even rejected. Remember, walls between spaces change color temporarily when properly aligned.

- Make liberal use of the *zoom* tool for sizing and aligning components accurately. Zoom in as closely as possible on the area being worked. When aligning objects, it is also helpful to use the full-screen cursor.

- Turn on the grid and verify spacing. This makes it easier to align objects and get a sense of the sizes of objects and the distances between them. Use the *measure* tool to check exact measurements if needed.

- Make liberal use of the sketch tools. These can be turned on and off and do not count during the grading, but they can be used to show relationships and for temporary guidelines and other notations.

- Use sketch circles to show required distances, setbacks, clearances, and similar measures.

AFTER THE EXAM

When you've clicked the button to end the test, the computer may prompt you to provide some demographic information about yourself and your education and experience. Then gather your belongings, turn in your scratch paper and materials—you must leave them with the proctor—and leave the test site. (For security reasons, you can't remove anything from the test site.) If the staff has retained your Authorization to Test and your identification, don't forget to retrieve both.

If you should encounter any problems during the exam or have any concerns, be sure to report them to the test site administrator and to NCARB as soon as possible. If you wait longer than ten days after you test, NCARB will not respond to your complaint. You must report your complaint immediately and directly to NCARB and copy your state registration board for any hope of assistance.

Then it's all over but the wait for the mail. How long it takes to get your scores will vary with the efficiency of your state registration board, which reviews the scores from NCARB before passing along the results. But four to six weeks is typical.

As you may have heard from classmates and colleagues, the ARE is a difficult exam—but it is certainly not impossible to pass. A solid architectural education and a well-rounded internship are the best preparation you can have. Watch carefully and listen to the vocabulary used by architects with more experience. Look for opportunities to participate in all phases of project delivery so that you have some "real world" experience to apply to the scenarios you will inevitably find on the exam.

One last piece of advice is not to put off taking the exams. Take them as soon as you become eligible. You will probably still remember a little bit from your college courses and you may even have your old textbooks and notes handy. As life gets more complicated—with spouses and children and work obligations—it is easy to make excuses and never find time to get around to it. Make the commitment, and do it now. After all, this is the last step to reaching your goal of calling yourself an architect.

HOW TO USE THIS BOOK

This book contains 123 sample multiple-choice problems and one sample vignette, as well as one complete practice exam consisting of 95 multiple-choice problems and one vignette. These have been written to help you prepare for the Building Systems division of the Architect Registration Examination.

One of the best ways to prepare for the ARE is by solving sample problems. While you are studying for this division, use the sample problems in this book to make yourself familiar with the different types of problems and the breadth of topics you are likely to encounter on the actual exam. Then when it's time to take the ARE, you will already be comfortable with the format of the exam problems. Also, seeing which sample problems you can and cannot answer correctly will help you gauge your understanding of the topics covered in the Building Systems division.

The sample multiple-choice problems in this book are organized by subject area, so that you can concentrate on one subject at a time if you like. Each problem is immediately followed by its answer and an explanation.

The sample vignette in this book can be solved directly on the base plan provided or on a sheet of tracing paper. Alternatively, you can download an electronic file of the base plan in PDF format from **www.ppi2pass.com/vignettes** for use in your own CAD program. (On the actual exam, vignettes are solved on the computer using NCARB's own software; see the Introduction for more information about this.) When you are finished with your solution to the vignette, compare it against the sample passing and failing solutions that follow.

While the sample problems in this book are intended for you to use as you study for the exam, the practice exam is best used only when you have almost finished your study of the Building Systems topics. A week or two before you are scheduled to take the division, when you feel you are nearly ready for the exam, do a "dry run" by taking the practice

exam in this book. This will hone your test-taking skills and give you a reality check about how prepared you really are.

The experience will be most valuable to you if you treat the practice exam as though it were an actual exam. Do not read the problems ahead of time and do not look at the solutions until after you've finished. Try to simulate the exam experience as closely as possible. This means locking yourself away in a quiet space, setting an alarm for the exam's testing time, and working through the entire practice exam with no coffee, television, or telephone—only your calculator, a pencil, your drafting tools or CAD program for the vignette, and a few sheets of scratch paper. (On the actual exam, the CAD program, an on-screen calculator, scratch paper, and pencils are provided.) This will help you prepare to budget your time, give you an idea of what the actual exam experience will be like, and help you develop a test-taking strategy that works for you.

The target times for the sections of the practice exam are

Multiple choice: 2 hours

Mechanical and Electrical Plan vignette: 1 hour

Within the time allotted for each section, you may work on the problems or vignette in any order and spend any amount of time on each one.

Record your answers for the multiple-choice section of the practice exam using the "bubble" answer form at the front of the exam. When you are finished, you can check your answers quickly against the filled-in answer key at the front of the Solutions section. Then turn to the solutions and read the explanations of the answers, especially those you answered incorrectly. The explanation will give you a better understanding of the intent of the problem and why individual options are right or wrong.

The Solutions section may also be used as a guide for the final phase of your studies. As opposed to a traditional study guide that is organized into chapters and paragraphs of facts, this problem-and-solution format can help you see how the exam might address a topic, and what types of problems you are likely to encounter. If you still are not clear about a particular subject after reading a solution's explanation, review the subject in one of your study resources. Give yourself time for further study, and then take the multiple-choice section again.

The vignette portion of the practice exam can be solved the same way as the sample vignette, either directly on the base plan, on tracing paper, or with a CAD program using the electronic files downloaded from **www.ppi2pass.com/ vignettes**. Try to solve the vignette within the target time given. When you are finished, compare your drawing against the passing and failing solutions given in the Solutions section.

This book is best used in conjunction with your primary study source or study guide, such as PPI's *ARE Review Manual*. *Building Systems: ARE Sample Problems and Practice Exam* is not intended to give you all the information you will need to pass this division of the ARE. Rather, it is designed to expose you to a variety of problem types and to help you sharpen your problem-solving and test-taking skills. With a sound review and the practice you'll get from this book, you'll be well on your way to successfully passing the Building Systems division of the Architect Registration Examination.

HOW SI UNITS ARE USED IN THIS BOOK

This book includes equivalent measurements in the text and illustrations using the Système International (SI), or the *metric system* as it is commonly called. However, the use of SI units for construction and book publishing in the United States is problematic. This is because the building construction industry in the United States (with the exception of federal construction) has generally not adopted the metric system. As a result, equivalent measurements of customary U.S. units (also called English or inch-pound units) are usually given as a *soft* conversion, in which customary U.S. measurements are simply converted into SI units using standard conversion factors. This always results in a number with excessive significant digits. When construction is done using SI units, the building is designed and drawn according to *hard* conversions, where planning dimensions and building products are based on a metric module from the beginning. For example, studs are spaced 400 mm on center to accommodate panel products that are manufactured in standard 1200 mm widths.

During the present time of transition to the Système International in the United States, code-writing bodies, federal laws such as the ADA and the ABA, product manufacturers, trade associations, and other construction-related industries typically still use the customary U.S. system and make soft conversions to develop SI equivalents. Some manufacturers produce the same products in sizes for each measuring system. Although there are industry standards for developing SI equivalents, there is no perfect consistency for rounding off when conversions are made. For example, the *International Building Code* shows a 152 mm equivalent when a 6 in dimension is required, while the *Americans with Disabilities Act and Architectural Barriers Act Accessibility Guidelines* (*ADA/ABA Guidelines*) give a 150 mm equivalent for the same customary U.S. dimension.

To further complicate matters, each book publisher may employ a slightly different house style in handling SI equivalents when customary U.S. units are used as the primary measuring system. The confusion is likely to continue until the United States construction industry adopts the SI system completely, eliminating the need for dual dimensioning in publishing.

For the purposes of this book, the following conventions have been adopted.

Throughout the book, the customary U.S. measurements are given first with the SI equivalent shown in parentheses. When the measurement is millimeters, units are not shown. For example, a dimension may be indicated as 4 ft 8 in (1422). When the SI equivalent is some other unit, such as for volume or area, the units are indicated. For example, 250 ft² (23 m²).

Following standard conventions, all SI distance measurements in illustrations are in millimeters unless specifically indicated as meters.

When a measurement is given as part of a problem scenario, the SI measurement is not necessarily meant to be roughly equal to the U.S. measurement. For example, a hypothetical force on a beam might be given as 12 kips (12 kN). 12 kips is actually equal to about 53.38 kN, but the intention in such cases is only to provide two problems, one in U.S. units and one in SI units, of about the same difficulty. Solve the entire problem in either U.S. or SI units; don't try to convert from one to the other in the middle of solving a problem.

When dimensions are for informational use, the SI equivalent rounded to the nearest millimeter is used.

When dimensions are given and they relate to planning or design guidelines, the SI equivalent is rounded to the nearest 5 mm for numbers over a few inches and to the nearest 10 mm for numbers over a few feet. When the dimension exceeds several feet, the number is rounded to the nearest 100 mm. For example, if you need a space about 10 ft wide for a given activity, the modular, rounded SI equivalent will be given as 3000 mm. More exact conversions are not required.

When an item is only manufactured to a customary U.S. measurement, the nearest SI equivalent rounded to the nearest millimeter is given, unless the dimension is very small (as for metal gages), in which case a more precise decimal equivalent will be given. Some materials, such as glass, are often manufactured to SI sizes. So, for example, a nominal $^1/_2$ in thick piece of glass will have an SI equivalent of 13 mm but can be ordered as 12 mm.

When there is a hard conversion in the industry and an SI equivalent item is manufactured, the hard conversion is given. For example, a 24 × 24 ceiling tile would have the hard conversion of 600 × 600 (instead of 610) because these are manufactured and available in the United States.

When an SI conversion is used by a code, such as the *International Building Code*, or published in another regulation, such as the *ADA/ABA Guidelines*, the SI equivalents used by the issuing agency are printed in this book. For example, the same 10 ft dimension given previously as 3000 mm for a planning guideline would have an SI equivalent of 3048 mm in the context of the IBC because this is what that code requires. The *ADA/ABA Guidelines* generally follow the rounding rule, to take SI dimensions to the nearest 10 mm. For example, a 10 ft requirement for accessibility will be shown as 3050 mm. The code requirements for readers outside the United States may be slightly different.

This book uses different abbreviations for pounds of force and pounds of mass in customary U.S. units. The abbreviation used for pounds of force (pounds-force) is lbf, and the abbreviation used for pounds of mass (pounds-mass) is lbm.

CODES AND STANDARDS USED IN THIS BOOK

ADA/ABA Guidelines: *Americans with Disabilities Act and Architectural Barriers Act Accessibility Guidelines*, 2005. U.S. Architectural and Transportation Barriers Compliance Board, Washington, DC.

ANSI/ASHRAE 62.1-2007: *Ventilation for Acceptable Indoor Air Quality*, 2007. American Society of Heating, Refrigerating and Air-Conditioning Engineers, Atlanta, GA.

ANSI/ASHRAE/IESNA 90.1-2007: *Energy Standard for Buildings Except Low-Rise Residential Buildings*, 2007. American Society of Heating, Refrigerating and Air-Conditioning Engineers, Atlanta, GA.

IBC: *International Building Code*, 2009. International Code Council, Washington, DC.

ICC/ANSI A117.1-2003, *Accessible and Usable Buildings and Facilities*, 2003. International Code Council. Washington, DC.

IPC: *International Plumbing Code*, 2009. International Code Council, Washington, DC.

LEED 2009: Leadership in Energy and Environmental Design (LEED) 2009 Green Building Rating System for New Construction. U.S. Green Building Council, Washington, DC.

NEC (NFPA 70): *National Electrical Code*, 2008. National Fire Protection Association, Quincy, MA.

NFPA 10: *Standard for Portable Fire Extinguishers*, 2010. National Fire Protection Association, Quincy, MA.

RECOMMENDED READING

General Reference

ARCOM. *MasterSpec*. Salt Lake City: ARCOM. (Familiarity with the format and language of specifications is very helpful.)

ARCOM and American Institute of Architects. *The Graphic Standards Guide to Architectural Finishes: Using MasterSpec to Evaluate, Select, and Specify Materials*. Hoboken, NJ: John Wiley & Sons.

Ballast, David Kent, and Steven E. O'Hara. *ARE Review Manual*. Belmont, CA: Professional Publications, Inc.

Fitch, James Marston. *Historic Preservation: Curatorial Management of the Built World*. Charlottesville: University Press of Virginia.

Guthrie, Pat. *Architect's Portable Handbook*. New York: McGraw-Hill.

Harris, Cyril M., ed. *Dictionary of Architecture and Construction*. New York: McGraw-Hill.

Mahoney, William D. *ADA/ABA Handbook: Accessibility Guidelines for Buildings and Facilities*. East Providence, RI: BNI Building News.

Ramsey, Charles G., and Harold R. Sleeper. *Architectural Graphic Standards*. Hoboken, NJ: John Wiley & Sons. (The student edition is an acceptable substitute for the professional version.)

U.S. Green Building Council. *LEED Reference Package for New Construction and Major Renovations*. Washington, DC: U.S. Green Building Council.

Building Systems

American Institute of Architects. *Environmental Resource Guide*. Washington, DC: American Institute of Architects.

Allen, Edward, and Joseph Iano. *The Architect's Studio Companion*. Hoboken, NJ: John Wiley & Sons. (The "Designing Spaces for Mechanical and Electrical Services" section provides a very good comparison of advantages and applications for types of systems.)

Brown, G. Z., and Mark DeKay. *Sun, Wind, and Light: Architectural Design Strategies*. Hoboken, NJ: John Wiley & Sons.

Cavanaugh, William J., and Joseph A. Wilkes, eds. *Architectural Acoustics: Principles and Practice*. Hoboken, NJ: John Wiley & Sons.

Cowan, James. *Architectural Acoustics Design Guide*. New York: McGraw-Hill.

Egan, M. David, and Victor Olgyay. *Architectural Lighting*. New York: McGraw-Hill.

Guzowski, Mary. *Daylighting for Sustainable Design*. New York: McGraw-Hill Professional Publishing.

Kristensen, Poul, and Roman Jacobiak, eds. *Daylight in Buildings*. Hoboken, NJ: John Wiley & Sons.

Lechner, Norbert. *Heating, Cooling, Lighting: Design Methods for Architects*. Hoboken, NJ: John Wiley & Sons.

Patterson, James. *Simplified Design for Building Fire Safety*. Hoboken, NJ: John Wiley & Sons.

Rush, Richard. *The Buildings Systems Integration Handbook*. Woburn, MA: Butterworth-Heinemann.

Steffy, Gary. *Architectural Lighting Design*. Hoboken, NJ: John Wiley & Sons.

Stein, Benjamin. *Building Technology: Mechanical and Electrical Systems*. Hoboken, NJ: John Wiley & Sons.

Stein, Benjamin, et al. *Mechanical and Electrical Equipment for Buildings*. Hoboken, NJ: John Wiley & Sons.

Graphic Vignettes

Allen, Edward, and Joseph Iano. *The Architect's Studio Companion: Rules of Thumb for Preliminary Design*. Hoboken, NJ: John Wiley & Sons.

Ambrose, James, and Peter Brandow. *Simplified Site Design*. Hoboken, NJ: John Wiley & Sons.

Ching, Francis D.K., and Steven R. Winkel. *Building Codes Illustrated: A Guide to Understanding the International Building Code*. Hoboken, NJ: John Wiley & Sons.

Hoke, John Ray, ed. *Architectural Graphic Standards*. Hoboken, NJ: John Wiley & Sons.

Karlen, Mark. *Space Planning Basics*. Hoboken, NJ: John Wiley & Sons.

Parker, Harry, John W. MacGuire, and James Ambrose. *Simplified Site Engineering*. Hoboken, NJ: John Wiley & Sons.

Architectural History

(Brush up on this before taking any of the multiple-choice exams, as architectural history problems are scattered throughout the sections.)

Curtis, William J.R. *Modern Architecture Since 1900*. London: Phaedon Press, Ltd.

Frampton, Kenneth. *Modern Architecture: A Critical History*. London: Thames and Hudson.

Trachtenberg, Marvin, and Isabelle Hyman. *Architecture: From Pre-History to Post-Modernism*. Englewood Cliffs, NJ: Prentice-Hall.

SAMPLE PROBLEMS

CODES AND REGULATIONS

1. Emergency lighting in means-of-egress areas must have an intensity of no less than _____ fc (_____ lx). (Fill in the blank.)

Solution

Building codes require a minimum of 1 fc (11 lx) at the floor level for areas that serve as a means of egress. For assembly occupancies, such as an auditorium or theater, the level may be reduced to 0.2 fc (2.15 lx) during performances, but must be automatically restored to 1 fc (11 lx) upon activation of the building's fire alarm system. Exceptions to the minimum requirement may include Group U occupancies, guest rooms in Group R-1 occupancies, dwelling units, and sleeping rooms in Groups R-2 and R-3 occupancies. Sleeping rooms in Group I occupancies are also exempt.

> *Study Note:* When artificial light is provided, 10 fc (107 lx) is the minimum lighting level permitted for the entire room at 30 in (762) above the floor.

Buildings must be provided with emergency energy sources to operate emergency lighting, exit signs, automatic door locks, and other equipment vital to life safety. These sources may include batteries or emergency generators. The sources of power must be capable of operating for 90 min or as modified by the local code.

The answer is 1 fc (11 lx).

2. Which of the following building types would have the most stringent requirements for fire alarm and fire suppression systems?

- A. motel
- B. nursing home
- C. office building
- D. print shop

Solution

As a Group I (institutional) occupancy, a nursing home would be required to have extensive alarm systems and be sprinklered throughout. Occupants of institutional buildings, such as hospitals, prisons, and nursing homes, often have limited mobility and require more warning and time to evacuate the building in case of fire.

Group B (business) occupancies, such as office buildings and print shops, are not required to be equipped with automatic sprinkler systems, and small Group B occupancies are not required to have alarm systems if the occupant load is low or if the sprinkler system is equipped with flow valves that activate an alarm when sprinkler water flows. Although a motel would be required to have smoke alarms, it probably would not be required to have a sprinkler system since motels are typically one or two stories high and each guest room has a doorway leading directly to an exterior exit access.

The answer is B.

3.   What type of sink is best for barrier-free design?

   A.   wall-hung
   B.   built-in
   C.   vanity
   D.   pedestal

Solution

All the sink installations listed as possible answers can work if they meet the measurement requirements shown, but a wall-hung lavatory gives the most open access, usually exceeding the minimum requirements shown here.

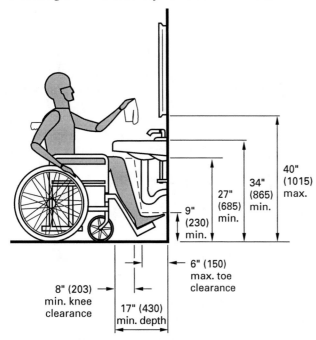

lavatory clearances

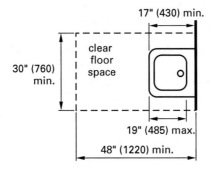

clear floor space at lavatories

The answer is A.

4.   Information regarding the minimum number of plumbing fixtures required for various occupancies may be found in which of the following sources?

   A.   building codes
   B.   plumbing codes
   C.   both building and plumbing codes
   D.   the local authority having jurisdiction

Solution

The required number of plumbing fixtures is given in plumbing codes. Often these requirements are also reproduced in the building codes.

The answer is C.

5.   The area of operable windows required in a naturally ventilated building is based on which of the following factors?

   A.   the number of required air changes per hour
   B.   a percentage of the floor area being ventilated
   C.   an area of opening given in the mechanical code
   D.   a minimum volume per minute given in ASHRAE standards

Solution

The area of operable windows required in a naturally ventilated building equals a percentage of the floor area being ventilated. The exact percentage varies with the code. The *International Building Code* requires that the minimum openable area to the outdoors be 4% of the floor area.

The answer is B.

6.   The minimum fresh air ventilation rate recommended by ANSI/ASHRAE 62.1 is

   A.   5 cfm/person (3 L/s/person)
   B.   10 cfm/person (5 L/s/person)
   C.   15 cfm/person (8 L/s/person)
   D.   20 cfm/person (10 L/s/person)

Solution

Although ventilation rates vary depending on the use of the space, 15 cfm/person (8 L/s/person) is the lowest rate recommended by ANSI/ASHRAE 62.1.

The answer is C.

7.   Standard accessible toilet stalls must have a clear width of at least

    A.   48 in (1220)
    B.   56 in (1420)
    C.   60 in (1525)
    D.   66 in (1675)

Solution

A standard accessible stall must be 60 in (1525) wide. Alternate designs for toilet stalls can be 36 in (915) or 48 in (1220) wide. Required dimensions are shown here.

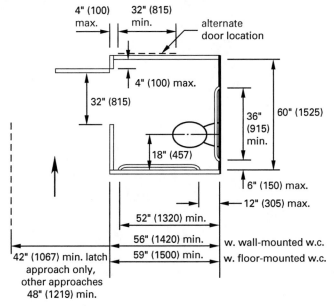

standard stall

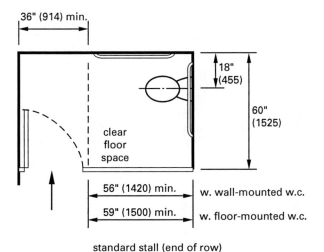

standard stall (end of row)

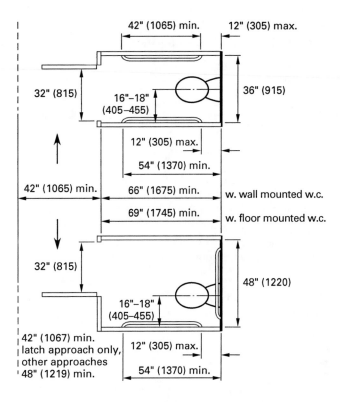

alternative toilet stall dimensions

The answer is C.

8.   In areas of unobstructed forward reach, light switches and thermostats may be located a maximum of

    A.   42 in (1067) above the finished floor
    B.   44 in (1118) above the finished floor
    C.   48 in (1220) above the finished floor
    D.   54 in (1372) above the finished floor

Solution

The *ADA/ABA Guidelines* permit a maximum forward high reach of 48 in (1220).

Study Note: The *ADA/ABA Guidelines* also allow a 54 in (1372) maximum distance for unobstructed side reach. However, the newer ICC/ANSI A117.1 allows just 48 in (1220) for both forward and side unobstructed reaches. The minimum low side reach dimension of 9 in (230) in the *ADA/ABA Guidelines* has also been changed in ICC/ANSI A117.1 to 15 in (380).

The answer is C.

9.   Which of the following types of standpipe connections are intended for use by building occupants?

    A.   Class I only
    B.   Class II only
    C.   Class I and Class II only
    D.   Class II and Class III only

Solution

Class II standpipes have $1^1/_2$ in (38) connections, with hoses intended to be used by building occupants. Class III standpipes have both $1^1/_2$ in (38) and $2^1/_2$ in (64) connections. The $1^1/_2$ in (38) connection of a Class III standpipe has an attached hose intended for use by building occupants, and the $2^1/_2$ in (64) connection is intended for use by firefighters.

A Class I standpipe is a dry standpipe system with only a $2^1/_2$ in (64) connection, intended exclusively for use by firefighters.

The answer is D.

10.   Which of the following members of the building team participate in the building commissioning process? (Choose the four that apply.)

    A.   civil engineer
    B.   electrical engineer
    C.   elevator contractor
    D.   interior designer
    E.   owner
    F.   mechanical engineer

Solution

The civil engineer and the interior designer typically would not participate in the building commissioning process because they do not have direct involvement in the design or operation of the building systems.

The answer is B, C, E, and F.

11.   Which of the following would have the greatest impact on the size and configuration of an accessible restroom?

    A.   a 5 ft (1525) clear circular turnaround space
    B.   maneuvering space on the outside of the entry door to the room
    C.   clear space at towel dispensers and full-height mirrors
    D.   a minimum 36 in (915) access route into and through the room

Solution

Providing for a 5 ft (1525) turning circle requires the most space of the four choices listed. If the turning circle is provided, it is very likely that a 36 in (915) access space and clear space at the towel dispensers will also be available. The maneuvering space on the outside of the entry door is irrelevent to the interior dimensions of the restroom.

The answer is A.

ENVIRONMENTAL ISSUES

12.   Heat loss in a building can be minimized by selecting wall materials with high

    A.   conductance
    B.   enthalpy
    C.   permeability
    D.   resistance

Solution

Resistance is the number of hours needed for 1 Btu to pass through 1 ft² of a material of a given thickness when the temperature differential is 1°F (the number of seconds needed for 1 J to pass through 1 m² of material of a given thickness when the temperature differential is 1°C). A higher resistance means that heat takes longer to pass through, and thus the material has greater insulation value.

Conductance is the reciprocal of resistance and is the rate of heat loss measured in Btu/hr (watts) through 1 ft² (1 m²) of a material of a given thickness when the temperature differential is 1°F (1°C). *Enthalpy* is the total heat in a substance, including latent heat and sensible heat. *Permeability* is the property of a porous material that permits the passage of water vapor through it.

The answer is D.

13.   Which of the following would NOT maximize daylighting while minimizing solar heat load?

    A.   horizontal shades
    B.   light shelves
    C.   tinted glass
    D.   building shape

Solution

Although tinted glass would reduce the heat load, it would not be good for maximizing daylighting. Instead, low-ε (low-emittance) glass or "super windows" with clear glazing would be more appropriate. All of the other choices would be good ways to minimize direct sunlight on the glass while improving transmitted light to the interior of the building.

The answer is C.

14. Which type of glass would be the most appropriate choice for a location in the northeastern United States?

    A. low-ε
    B. reflective
    C. tinted
    D. triple-pane

Solution

Low-ε (low-emittance) glass would be a good choice for a cold climate because it has a low U-value, which means that it can minimize heat loss while still allowing some solar heat gain. The low-ε film or coating allows both visible and near-infrared radiation to be transmitted through the glass but prevents long-wave radiation (heat) from escaping the room.

Reflective, tinted, and triple-pane glass is not as efficient as the newer technologies of low-ε glass or "super windows." Reflective and tinted glass would reduce heat gain in the summer but would not allow desirable heat gain during the cold months.

The answer is A.

15. The microclimate of a site around a building can be controlled by which two of the following factors?

  I. albedo
  II. conductivity
  III. orientation of the building
  IV. radiation

    A. I and II
    B. I and IV
    C. II and III
    D. III and IV

Solution

The *albedo* of a surface material is the fraction of the radiant energy received on the surface that is reflected. Surfaces with low albedo, like grass, absorb radiant energy. The *conductivity* of a material is the rate of heat flow through it. Albedo and conductivity combined can affect the microclimate around a building.

The *orientation of the building* does not affect microclimate to any appreciable degree, although it is important in daylighting design and design for passive solar heating. *Radiation* is the transmission of heat through space by means of electromagnetic waves. As such, radiation might heat a building due to a nearby hot surface, but not because of the air or climate around a building.

The answer is A.

16. The angle of the sun's orientation relative to due south is called the

    A. altitude
    B. azimuth
    C. declination
    D. solar angle

Solution

Azimuth is the angle of the orientation of the sun relative to due south.

Altitude is the angle of the sun relative to the horizon. *Declination* is the angle of the north-south axis of the earth relative to the sun. Solar angle is not a term in architectural design.

The answer is B.

17. It is desirable for an insulating material to have a high

    A. conductance
    B. conductivity
    C. enthalpy
    D. resistance

Solution

Insulating materials should possess a high level of *resistance*. Resistance is the number of hours it takes for 1 Btu to be transferred through 1 ft² of material when the temperature differential is 1°F (the number of seconds it takes for 1 J to be transferred through 1 m² of material when the temperature differential is 1°C), so a higher value is better.

The answer is D.

18.   Weatherstripping affects

    A.   effective temperature
    B.   thermodynamics
    C.   ventilation
    D.   infiltration

Solution

Weatherstripping helps seal joints and cracks around doors and windows, reducing air infiltration. Air infiltration is a primary factor in heat loss, so sealing these voids improves the performance of mechanical systems and conserves energy.

The answer is D.

19.   A roof covers an area 40 ft (12 m) wide and 80 ft (24 m) long. With heavy insulation, the resistance has been calculated as 38 ft²-hr-°F/Btu (6.7 m²·°C/W) and the design equivalent temperature difference is 44°F (24°C). The design temperature is −5°F (−20°C) and it is desired to maintain a 70°F (22°C) indoor temperature. The heat loss through the roof is most nearly

    A.   3700 Btu/hr (1100 W)
    B.   5500 Btu/hr (1600 W)
    C.   5800 Btu/hr (1700 W)
    D.   6200 Btu/hr (1800 W)

Solution

The design equivalent temperature difference has no bearing on the solution to this problem. First, calculate the U-value, which is the reciprocal of the R-value.

In U.S. units:

$$U = \frac{1}{R} = \frac{1}{38 \dfrac{\text{ft}^2\text{-hr-}°\text{F}}{\text{Btu}}}$$

$$= 0.026 \text{ Btu/ft}^2\text{-hr-}°\text{F}$$

In SI units:

$$U = \frac{1}{R} = \frac{1}{6.7 \dfrac{\text{m}^2\cdot°\text{C}}{\text{W}}}$$

$$= 0.15 \text{ W/m}^2\cdot°\text{C}$$

The temperature difference is

In U.S. units:

$$\Delta T = T_{\text{indoor}} - T_{\text{design}}$$
$$= 70°\text{F} - (-5°\text{F})$$
$$= 75°\text{F}$$

In SI units:

$$\Delta T = T_{\text{indoor}} - T_{\text{design}}$$
$$= 22°\text{C} - (-20°\text{C})$$
$$= 42°\text{C}$$

The roof area is 40 ft by 80 ft, or 3200 ft² (12 m by 24 m, or 288 m²). Determine the total heat loss.

In U.S. units:

$$q = U A \Delta T$$

$$= \left(0.026 \frac{\text{Btu}}{\text{ft}^2\text{-hr-}°\text{F}}\right)(3200 \text{ ft}^2)(75°\text{F})$$

$$= 6240 \text{ Btu/hr} \quad (6200 \text{ Btu/hr})$$

In SI units:

$$q = U A \Delta T$$

$$= \left(0.15 \frac{\text{W}}{\text{m}^2\cdot°\text{C}}\right)(288 \text{ m}^2)(42°\text{C})$$

$$= 1814.4 \text{ W} \quad (1800 \text{ W})$$

The answer is D.

20.   Melting ice consumes

    A.   enthalpy
    B.   sensible heat
    C.   dew-point temperature
    D.   latent heat

Solution

Latent heat is the heat needed to produce a change of state in a material. The addition of sensible heat is what raises the temperature, but at 32°F (0°C) the addition of more heat no longer immediately raises the temperature more. Instead, the added heat serves to melt the ice, and the temperature does not rise again until the ice is melted. The heat that is used to melt the ice rather than raise the temperature is latent heat.

The answer is D.

21. What would be the best passive cooling strategy during the summer in a hot-humid climate?

    A. Design a series of pools and fountains to cool by evaporation.
    B. Include broad overhangs to shield glass and outdoor activities from the sun.
    C. Orient the building to catch summer breezes.
    D. Use light-colored surfaces to reflect sunlight and reduce solar gain.

Solution

When the temperature is above about 85°F (29°C), the body loses more heat through evaporation than through convection or radiation. In a humid climate this process is retarded, so encouraging air movement would be the best strategy. Overhangs and light-colored surfaces would help minimize heat buildup in the structure itself, and water features contribute to a feeling of comfort by cooling through evaporation and having a psychological cooling effect.

The answer is C.

22. The Indian Pueblo in Taos, New Mexico, illustrates which of the following climatic design principles?

    A. daylighting
    B. sun shading
    C. volume utilization
    D. wind effect

Solution

The adobe buildings in the Taos Indian Pueblo were built in cubic shapes. Among all solid shapes made of rectangles, a cube gives the greatest volume for the least amount of surface area, thus minimizing heat gain in the summer.

There is little *sun shading* provided, but the pueblos do utilize very small windows to minimize heat gain by admitting little sunlight, which makes *daylighting* inappropriate. Cooling by *wind effect* would require long, narrow buildings with many openings.

The answer is C.

23. The greatest degree of protection from cold winter winds can be achieved with

    A. airlocks
    B. earth sheltering
    C. green roofs
    D. landscaping

Solution

Earth sheltering would offer the greatest degree of protection from cold winter winds. *Airlocks* only protect door openings. *Green roofs* are primarily used to protect against solar radiation and to reduce runoff. *Landscaping* can reduce the negative effects of wind, but not as well as solid earth.

The answer is B.

24. The best measure to use when evaluating how well a window assembly prevents heat gain is the

    A. daylight factor
    B. shading coefficient
    C. solar heat gain coefficient
    D. window-to-wall ratio

Solution

The *solar heat gain coefficient* is the ratio of solar heat gain through a window to the amount of solar radiation striking the window. Because it includes the frame and the glass spacer, the solar heat gain coefficient is a better indicator of heat gain than the *shading coefficient*, which is a similar measure but does not include the effects of the frame. The *daylight factor* and the *window-to-wall ratio* are not measures of heat gain.

The answer is C.

25. A ground-source heat pump would NOT be appropriate

    A. on a site with extensive subsurface rock
    B. for a midsize commercial building
    C. for multifamily housing
    D. in a hot-arid climatic region

Solution

Because ground-source heat pumps require an extensive network of buried vertical or horizontal piping, a rocky site would make the installation prohibitively expensive.

The answer is A.

26. A massive brick wall behind glazing on the south side of a house would act as a

- A. direct gain system
- B. greenhouse design
- C. passive system with active assist
- D. Trombe wall

Solution

A *Trombe wall* is a type of thermal storage wall that is placed directly behind glass on the south side of a building to store solar energy during the day for release at night.

A *direct gain system* uses various types of massive materials (masonry, concrete, or even gypsum board) in various locations inside a building to store heat. A *greenhouse* uses a south-facing room enclosed with extensive glass, not masonry. A *passive system with active assist* includes mechanical devices in addition to thermal mass.

The answer is D.

27. The apparent angle of the sun above the horizon is the

- A. altitude
- B. azimuth
- C. declination
- D. latitude

Solution

The apparent angle of the sun above the horizon is the *altitude*. Both altitude and *azimuth* describe the location of the sun in relationship to a specific point on the earth. Azimuth expresses the sun's compass orientation.

Declination is the angle of the earth's axis relative to the position of the sun. *Latitude* and *longitude* are used to express specific points on the earth.

The answer is A.

28. Wood chips and sawdust made into panel products are examples of

- A. post-consumer materials
- B. post-industrial materials
- C. recycled products
- D. renewable products

Solution

Post-industrial materials are by-products of manufacturing processes which can be integrated into other products. *Post-consumer materials* are those that have served their intended use. *Recycled products* are finished materials or products that have been either reused as they are or converted into another material. *Renewable materials* are components that can be grown or naturally replenished faster than humans can deplete it.

The answer is B.

29. Which of the following agricultural products is NOT a rapidly renewable material used in the production of panel products?

- A. bagasse
- B. poplar
- C. rice straw
- D. wheat straw

Solution

Bagasse (the residue from the processing of sugar cane) and rice straw are both alternative agricultural products that are made into panel products. Wheat straw is a little more common and is also used for straw particleboard. Poplar is a hardwood and is not rapidly renewable.

The answer is B.

30. An architect is evaluating the attributes of a particular building product as they relate to sustainability. The architect would most likely use

- A. an environmental impact study
- B. a life-cycle assessment
- C. an impact assessment
- D. a matrix comparison chart

Solution

A *life-cycle assessment* evaluates the environmental impact of a particular material over its entire useful life, including disposal. It could be used to compare the impacts of two or more materials so the architect could select the most sustainable one.

An *environmental impact study*, or EIS, is used to evaluate the impact of a development on the environment. An *impact assessment* is one phase of a life-cycle assessment. There is no sustainability evaluation method by the name "matrix comparison chart."

The answer is B.

31. Which of the following programs is used to evaluate only carpet products?

    A. CRI Green Label IAQ Program
    B. Greenguard Registry
    C. Green Seal Standards
    D. South Coast Air Quality Management District Rules

Solution

The Carpet and Rug Institute's (CRI) Green Label Indoor Air Quality (IAQ) Test Program evaluates carpet and carpet padding. A building may receive a LEED credit for using a carpet system that meets or exceeds these requirements. The product may be listed on the Greenguard Registry or have a Green Seal label, but neither of these programs evaluates only carpet products. The South Coast Air Quality Management District (SCAQMD) Rules set standards for VOC content of adhesives and sealants.

The answer is A.

32. Spray-on fireproofing and insulation containing asbestos are likely to be found only in buildings constructed before

    A. 1968
    B. 1970
    C. 1973
    D. 1978

Solution

The Environmental Protection Agency (EPA) banned the spray application of asbestos-containing fireproofing and insulation materials in 1973.

The answer is C.

33. Certified contractors are required for handling or abatement of all of the following hazardous materials EXCEPT

    A. asbestos
    B. lead
    C. PCBs
    D. radon

Solution

Radon detection and remediation can be done by anyone, from homeowners to specialty contractors. Asbestos, lead, and PCBs all must be handled by a certified contractor.

The answer is D.

34. A building that carries a "gold" rating has been designed and certified under

    A. Greenguard
    B. Green Seal
    C. ISO 14000
    D. LEED

Solution

The U.S. Green Building Council's (USGBC) *Leadership in Energy and Environmental Design* (LEED) Green Building Rating System certifies entire buildings that meet the program's prerequisites and achieve a specified number of credits. There are four levels of project certification that are based on the number of points achieved: certified (40-49 points), silver (50-59 points), gold (60-79 points), and platinum (80 points and above).

Greenguard and *Green Seal* are both product rating systems; Greenguard certifies products with acceptable emission levels, while Green Seal certifies products that meet certain environmental standards, including stringent limits of volatile organic compounds (VOCs). *ISO 14000* refers to the International Standards Organization's collection of standards and guidelines that relate to a variety of environmental standards, including labeling, life-cycle assessment, and others. ISO standards are used as a measure of performance for other organizations that certify products and make other environmental claims.

The answer is D.

35. Storm runoff is best minimized with the use of

    A. cisterns
    B. pervious paving
    C. riprap
    D. silt fences

Solution

Pervious paving allows rainwater to soak into the ground while providing support for parking or other outdoor activities.

Cisterns are designed for holding rainwater for further use, not to minimize the runoff. *Riprap* is stone reinforcement for the banks of rivers or lakes. *Silt fences* are used to prevent erosion and sediment runoff during construction.

The answer is B.

36. Which of these is used to determine the required size of a leaching field?

    A. percolation test
    B. yield test
    C. aquifer test
    D. water table test

Solution

The required size of a leaching field is determined by the quantity of effluent that must be accommodated and the ability of the soil to let the effluent soak in. This permeability of the soil is measured by the *percolation test*. None of the other options test either quantity or permeability.

The answer is A.

37. Which strategy will most effectively reduce stormwater runoff from a site?

    A. Capture rainwater for irrigation and other non-potable uses.
    B. Reduce the amount of impervious area.
    C. Construct a garden roof.
    D. Construct an on-site stormwater treatment facility.

Solution

Reducing the impervious area on a site is the most effective way to reduce stormwater runoff. *Impervious area* is any area of building or paving that does not allow stormwater to seep into the ground.

Though less effective, installing a garden roof is also a way to reduce stormwater runoff. Reusing captured rainwater for other approved uses, such as flushing toilets and irrigating landscaping, is a good way to manage stormwater and keep it on site. An on-site treatment facility would help remove contaminants from stormwater before it is released into nearby rivers or streams, but would not reduce stormwater runoff.

The answer is B.

38. Which of the following is NOT a type of shading device?

    A. loggia
    B. brise-soleil
    C. engawa
    D. belvedere

Solution

Shading elements have been used in all types of architecture around the world to help to mitigate the effects of the hot sun. The Greeks used porticos, the Japanese employed *engawas*, and twentieth-century designers such as Le Corbusier added *brise-soleils* to their designs. The deep overhangs on Frank Lloyd Wright's Robie House serve the same purpose as the veranda on a plantation house in the deep south. *Loggias*, colonnades, porches, galleries, and arcades are all devices that help to block the sun in the summer and can be designed to admit the sun when it is welcomed in the winter.

A *belvedere* is not a shading device. It is a small tower placed on the top of a building and used primarily as a lookout point. When fitted with operable windows and placed over a vertical opening through the building (such as a stair tower), it can also be used as an outlet for hot air rising to the ceiling through stack effect.

The answer is D.

39. Which of the following materials, in a layer 1 in (25) thick, will have the lowest *R*-value?

    A. snow
    B. air (with foil on both sides of the airspace)
    C. batt fiberglass insulation
    D. concrete

Solution

Good insulators have high *R*-values. Concrete has the lowest *R*-value and is the least effective insulator of the materials listed. Snow is actually a better insulator than concrete. Batt insulation is next, followed by the airspace with the reflective surfaces.

The answer is D.

PLUMBING

40. The surface of a water tank is 100 ft (30.5 m) above the lowest plumbing fixture in a building. Ignore friction loss. The water pressure available at the lowest fixture is most nearly

    A. 23 psi (163 kPa)
    B. 31 psi (220 kPa)
    C. 36 psi (255 kPa)
    D. 43 psi (305 kPa)

Solution

0.433 psi (10 kPa) is required to lift water a vertical distance of 1 ft (1 m). Viewed another way, 0.433 psi (10 kPa) of pressure is developed for every 1 ft (1 m) of height. This is called the *static head*. To determine the static head in this problem, use the following formula.

In U.S. units:

$$\text{pressure} = \left(0.433 \frac{\frac{\text{lbf}}{\text{in}^2}}{\text{ft}}\right)h$$

$$= \left(0.433 \frac{\frac{\text{lbf}}{\text{in}^2}}{\text{ft}}\right)(100 \text{ ft})$$

$$= 43.3 \text{ lbf}/\text{in}^2 \quad (43 \text{ psi})$$

In SI units:

$$\text{pressure} = \left(10 \frac{\text{kPa}}{\text{m}}\right)h$$

$$= \left(10 \frac{\text{kPa}}{\text{m}}\right)(30.5 \text{ m})$$

$$= 305 \text{ kPa}$$

Study Note: Another way to view the relationship is to remember that 1 psi will lift water 2.3 ft (10 kPa will lift water 1 m).

The answer is D.

41.   Which of the following types of copper pipe is most commonly used for supply lines in building plumbing systems?

A.   Type DWV
B.   Type K
C.   Type L
D.   Type M

Solution

Type L is the most commonly used copper pipe for building supply lines.

Type K is the heaviest type of copper pipe and is normally used as underground supply pipe. Type M is the thinnest of the K, L, M series and is only used where low pressure is involved, not for supply systems. Type DWV is only used for drainage, waste, and vent piping that is not subjected to the pressure level sustained by supply piping.

Study Note: In addition to copper pipe types, know the various types of plastic pipe designations and the circumstances under which they are used.

The answer is C.

42.   Which factor is dependent on building height?

A.   calculation of fixture units
B.   size of pressure tank
C.   determination of static head
D.   capacity of the submersible pump

Solution

The *static head* is determined by building height.

The answer is C.

43.   Which of the following domestic water heating systems would yield the lowest operating costs for a duplex residential unit?

A.   active closed-loop solar
B.   direct-fired storage tank
C.   ground-source heat pump
D.   tankless instantaneous

Solution

A solar water heating system would have the lowest long-term operating cost because no fuel costs would be involved.

A standard direct-fired storage tank unit would require purchasing gas, oil, or some other type of fuel to heat the water. A ground-source heat pump would not be able to supply water hot enough for domestic use and is inappropriate for this application; ground-source heat pumps are used for heating the home, not water. A tankless instantaneous unit would incur ongoing expenses due to its use of electricity and is not appropriate for general household domestic hot water generation.

The answer is A.

44. Which of the water heaters shown would be the LEAST efficient for domestic use?

A.

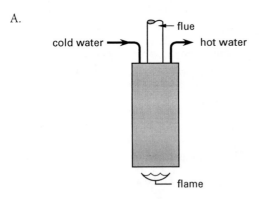

B.

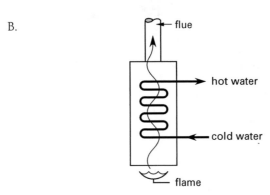

C.

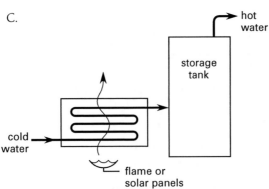

D.

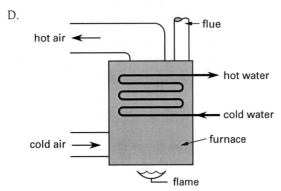

Solution

Option D illustrates an indirect, tankless type of water heating system. Water is heated in a furnace or boiler whose primary purpose is to provide space heating for the building. Therefore, to maintain desired quantities of hot water at all times, the furnace would have to operate during warm periods when space heating is not required. Generally, this type of heating system is used in conjunction with another source of heating for the water only. The furnace only provides hot water when it is operating to heat the building.

The answer is D.

45. The pressure in a city water main is 57 psi (390 kPa). The pressure loss through piping, fittings, and the water meter has been calculated as 23 psi (160 kPa), and the highest fixture requires 12 psi (80 kPa) to operate. What is the maximum height the fixture can be above the water main?

    A. 9 ft (2.7 m)
    B. 24 ft (7.2 m)
    C. 50 ft (15 m)
    D. 78 ft (24 m)

Solution

In order to find the maximum height, first take the pressure in the water main and subtract other known pressure losses and the pressure required for the fixture to operate properly.

In U.S. units:

$$57 \frac{\text{lbf}}{\text{in}^2} - 23 \frac{\text{lbf}}{\text{in}^2} - 12 \frac{\text{lbf}}{\text{in}^2} = 22 \text{ psi}$$

Because 1 psi is needed to lift water 2.3 ft, the maximum height is

$$\left(22 \frac{\text{lbf}}{\text{in}^2}\right)\left(2.3 \frac{\text{ft}}{\frac{\text{lbf}}{\text{in}^2}}\right) = 50.6 \text{ ft}$$

In SI units:

$$390 \text{ kPa} - 160 \text{ kPa} - 80 \text{ kPa} = 150 \text{ kPa}$$

Because 10 kPa is needed to lift water 1 m, the maximum height is

$$(150 \text{ kPa})\left(\frac{1 \text{ m}}{10 \text{ kPa}}\right) = 15 \text{ m}$$

The answer is C.

46. A drainage system for a small two-story building is shown.

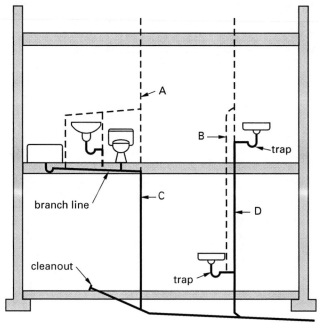

Which of the following components of the diagram is the stack vent?

  A. component A
  B. component B
  C. component C
  D. component D

Solution

The *stack vent* is the vent through the roof that connects directly to the uppermost part of a soil stack or a waste stack. Generally, other vent lines are connected to it *above* the branch line from the highest fixtures in the building.

  Terms to Know

  soil stack: a drainage pipe that serves a toilet

  vent stack: a vent that is separate from the soil or waste stack. A vent stack is typically used to vent fixtures below the topmost fixture in a building.

  waste stack: a pipe that serves only sinks and the like without being connected to a toilet

The answer is A.

47. Which of these is the most important concern in relation to a private water supply?

  A. fixture pressure
  B. hardness
  C. friction loss
  D. yield

Solution

Hardness affects the quality and taste of water as well as the longevity of the plumbing system. Very hard water can deposit minerals that build up in pipes and on plumbing fixtures. The taste may be objectionable, requiring installation of a water-softening or filtration system.

The answer is B.

48. Select the correct statements. (Choose the four that apply.)

  A. Dry-pipe sprinkler systems are more efficient than wet-pipe systems.
  B. Siamese connections serve both sprinklers and standpipes.
  C. The hazard classification does not necessarily affect sprinkler layout.
  D. Standpipes must be provided within stairways or within vestibules of smokeproof enclosures.
  E. Standpipes are required in buildings four or more stories high and those exceeding 150 ft.
  F. Sprinkler piping can be either copper or plastic.

Solution

The type of sprinkler system specified has nothing to do with its efficiency. Sprinkler spacing is always dependent on which hazard classification exists.

The answer is B, D, E, and F.

49. A graywater system would most appropriately be integrated into a

  A. laundromat
  B. office building
  C. residence
  D. restaurant

Solution

Graywater systems, when allowed by local building and
health departments, are most appropriately used where the
ratio of nonpotable to potable water needs is relatively high.
A laundromat would produce a great amount of wastewater
that could be captured for other purposes. A graywater system captures wastewater—for example, from lavatories,
washing machines, and other fixtures—that does not contain organic waste. The system then uses the water for irre-
gation or for nonpotable uses like flushing toilets.

The answer is A.

50.   A house is being designed for a new development in
a suburban location. The nearest water main is one block
away, about 300 ft (90 m), and the city currently has no
plans to extend the line in the near future. City and county
regulations do permit the drilling of wells. What action
should the architect recommend to the client regarding the
water supply?

   A.   Estimate the cost of extending the municipal
        line, since the water quality is known and it
        would ensure a long-term supply. Consult with
        nearby property owners who plan to build in
        the area to see if they would be willing to share
        the cost of extending the line.

   B.   Drill a test bore to determine the depth, poten-
        tial yield, and water quality of a well, and com-
        pare this information with the cost of extending
        the municipal line.

   C.   Assist the owner in petitioning the city to accel-
        erate its plans for extending the water line to
        serve new development.

   D.   Consult with nearby property owners who use
        wells and with well drillers to estimate the
        depth and yield of wells in the area. Compare
        the estimated cost and feasibility of drilling
        with the feasibility of extending the municipal
        line at the owner's cost.

Solution

Even though the nearest water line is 300 ft (90 m) away,
the best recommendation would be to use city water, where
the quality and quantity are known and a long-term supply
is assured. Although nearby property owners might or
might not be willing to share the cost, the owner would still
be best advised to extend the line.

Drilling a test bore could help determine the depth, potential yield, and water quality, but would cost almost as much
as drilling a well.

Petitioning the city to extend the line would be time-
consuming and probably not successful if they had already
decided against it.

Asking nearby property owners who use wells about their
experience would yield useful information, but even if the
cost and water quality were acceptable, extending the
municipal line would still be the preferred course of action.

The answer is A.

51.   Which three statements about drainage are correct?

I.   Drains should always slope at a minimum of $1/8$ in/ft
      (10 mm/m).
II.   The vent stack extends through the roof.
III. Vents help prevent the drainage of water from traps.
IV.   The house drain cannot also serve as the building
      sewer.
V.   Cleanouts are always a necessary part of a drainage
      system.

   A.   I, II, and V
   B.   I, III, and IV
   C.   II, III, and V
   D.   III, IV, and V

Solution

The minimum slope of drains depends on the size of the
pipe. The vent stack may extend through the roof, but this
is not required. In many cases, the vent stack connects with
the stack vent above the highest fixture served by the stack.

The answer is D.

52.   Water hammer is most likely to occur when

   A.   the incorrect type of valve is used
   B.   water suddenly stops because the flow is turned
        off
   C.   expansion joints are not installed in water lines
   D.   water flows backward against a check valve

Solution

Water hammer occurs when a valve is suddenly turned off
and causes the water to stop, forcing the pipes to shake.

The answer is B.

53. One component of a plumbing system common to every building is a

    A. stack vent
    B. vent stack
    C. backflow preventer
    D. house trap

Solution

A *stack vent* extends a soil or waste stack to vent through the roof, and every stack must have one of these.

A *vent stack* is a separate vent connected to a waste or soil stack in a multistory building, so not every building has this. A *house trap* is not mandatory in many codes, and a *backflow preventer* is not required in many plumbing installations.

The answer is A.

54. Select the incorrect statement.

    A. Several types of plastic can be used for cold water piping, but only PVDC may be used for hot water supply (where allowed by local codes).
    B. Steel pipe is more labor intensive and requires more space in plumbing chases than copper pipe.
    C. Type M pipe is normally specified for most interior plumbing.
    D. ABS is suitable for water supply.

Solution

Type M copper pipe is only used for low-pressure piping. Type L is the one most commonly used in plumbing installations.

The answer is C.

HVAC

55. By what process does insulating glass lose heat?

    A. convection
    B. conduction
    C. conductance
    D. radiation

Solution

Heat loss and gain through glazing is complex and results from a combination of the effects of conduction, convection, and radiation. Insulating glass consists of two or more layers of glazing separated by an airspace. Therefore, most heat loss through insulating glass is through convection, not conduction. The air circulating within the glass picks up heat on the warm side and transfers it on the cold side where it is lost by conduction through the glass to the outside. Even if the airspace is evacuated, there is still some air present.

The answer is A.

56. A small one-story building in a temperate climate has been designed with its long side oriented to the south. If a southern view is not a concern, the best passive solar heating method would be

    A. direct gain space
    B. Trombe wall
    C. greenhouse
    D. convective loop

Solution

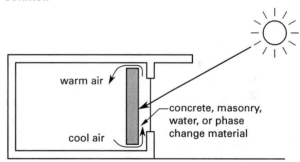

A *Trombe wall* is a type of thermal storage wall used in passive solar design. It uses mass to collect and store heat from the sun during the day. When heating is required, the stored heat in the mass is circulated by natural convection to the rest of the building. A Trombe wall is very efficient, but because it is positioned directly behind glass on the south side of a building, it blocks the view from inside the building.

If view is a consideration, a direct gain space, greenhouse, or convective loop using mass in the flooring and wall materials would be a better choice.

The answer is B.

57. Which HVAC system would be the most appropriate choice for a hospital?

    A. multizone
    B. high-velocity dual duct
    C. variable air volume
    D. fan coil with supplementary air

Solution

A system that exhausts all return air would be the best choice to maintain the quantities of fresh air needed in a hospital. A fan coil with supplementary air would satisfy this requirement.

All of the other systems listed return room air to the main air handling unit, where some of it is reused in the system.

The answer is D.

58. Which of the following contributors to indoor air quality can be controlled by the HVAC system? (Choose the four that apply.)

    A. outgassing
    B. air change effectiveness
    C. VOC content of building materials
    D. carbon dioxide levels
    E. humidity
    F. mold growth

Solution

Mechanical systems cannot control outgassing (the release of undesirable odors and chemicals) or the level of volatile organic compound (VOC) emissions from materials already incorporated into a building. These will exist regardless of the type of HVAC systems used. The HVAC system can provide continuous ventilation to remove VOCs and other undesirable chemicals from a building.

The HVAC system can control air change effectiveness and the levels of carbon dioxide found within the building. The HVAC system can also be relied on to keep humidity within human comfort range at acceptable levels to minimize mold growth.

The answer is B, D, E, and F.

59. Energy transfer wheels

    A. temper incoming air with exhaust air
    B. use ground temperature for heating or cooling
    C. capture the heat of flue gases to warm cold water
    D. exchange heat from solar panels to an airstream

Solution

An energy transfer wheel transfers heat between two airstreams (incoming air and exhaust air) using a lithium-chloride-impregnated heat exchanger. These devices transfer both latent and sensible heat and can be used to either heat or cool the incoming air.

Option B describes a ground-source heat pump. This type of system uses the constant temperature of the ground to heat or cool a building. Option C describes a boiler fuel economizer. Option D describes a standard heat exchanger.

Study Note: Understand the various types of mechanical techniques and devices used to conserve energy that are not necessarily active solar systems, photovoltaic systems, or wind systems. These include the economizer cycle, boil fuel economizers, heat pipes, runaround coils, energy transfer wheels, ground-source heat pumps, and dual-condenser chillers.

The answer is A.

60. Which of the following energy sources would be the most economical option for heating a small retail building in Washington state?

    A. electricity
    B. natural gas
    C. oil
    D. steam

Solution

In the northwestern part of the United States, electrical generating facilities are plentiful and provide a relatively low-cost way to heat buildings.

Natural gas is popular in the Midwest, while oil is commonly used in the northeastern part of the United States. Steam is not economical unless it is produced in a central facility for use in an urban area or is a by-product of other types of power generation.

The answer is A.

61. Which of the following have a significant effect on heat gain?

I. motors and equipment
II. sunlight
III. people
IV. fluorescent lighting
V. humidity

    A. II and III only
    B. II, III, and V only
    C. I, II, III, and IV only
    D. I, II, III, IV, and V

Solution

Humidity does not affect heat gain. Although the effect of motors and equipment, people, and lighting may vary in different types of occupancies, all the other factors listed produce heat.

The answer is C.

62. In calculating solar heat gain, what value must be known in addition to the area of the glass?

    A. mean radiant temperature
    B. design cooling factor
    C. equivalent temperature difference
    D. coefficient of heat transfer

Solution

The *design cooling factor* and the area of the glass must both be known to calculate solar heat gain.

Equivalent temperature difference is used to calculate heat gain through the building envelope, such as walls and roofs.

The answer is B.

63. Select the INCORRECT statement.

    A. Relative humidity is the best measure of thermal comfort.
    B. People feel more comfortable in the winter if the MRT is high.
    C. There are differences in comfort level among different cultural groups.
    D. The range of comfortable dry-bulb temperatures is dependent on air movement.

Solution

Although relative humidity affects the way a person feels in a space, it is not the primary measure of thermal comfort. *Effective temperature* (ET) is a better indicator of comfort because it takes all the variables into account. For example, even at a high humidity of 75%, if the temperature is cool enough or there is enough of a breeze, most people will feel comfortable.

The answer is A.

64. A developer in a midsize Arizona city is planning to build a small shopping mall for resale. The one-story mall will consist of 40,000 ft² (3700 m²) of rentable area surrounding a small enclosed courtyard. Existing utilities adjacent to the site include water, sanitary sewer, storm sewer, natural gas, and electricity. Which three of the following factors would be most important in the selection of an HVAC system for this project?

I. flexibility
II. climatic zone
III. economics
IV. the tenant's preference
V. building scale

    A. I, II, and V
    B. I, III, and IV
    C. II, III, and IV
    D. II, III, and V

Solution

The climatic zone, scale of the building, and cost and efficiency of the HVAC system would drive the specification. The shopping mall would be planned for relatively fixed sizes of rental spaces, so flexibility would not be one of the most important considerations. Because the tenant mix would probably not be completely known at the time of design, the tenant's preference could not be solicited even if it were appropriate.

The answer is D.

Illustration for Solutions 65 and 66.

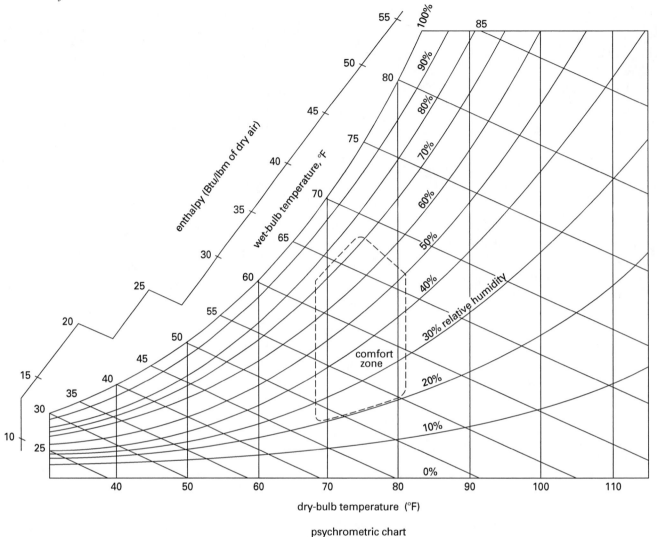

dry-bulb temperature (°F)

psychrometric chart

65. A sling psychrometer is primarily used to measure

    A. wet-bulb temperature
    B. dry-bulb temperature
    C. relative humidity
    D. the level of the dewpoint in humid climates

Solution

The *sling psychrometer* is a device used to measure wet-bulb temperature, which is then plotted on the psychrometric chart. Sling psychrometers often include a dry-bulb thermometer. Relative humidity can be determined from the difference between dry- and wet-bulb levels.

The answer is A.

66. The psychrometric chart CANNOT be used to

    A. plot the comfort zone
    B. design HVAC systems
    C. determine optimum ventilation rates
    D. determine the point of water condensation

Solution

The psychrometric chart is a graphical representation of air, heat, and moisture. It does not indicate or take into account the effects of air movement or ventilation rates on human comfort.

    Study Note: Review and understand the psychrometric chart and what the various line directions indicate. The exam may ask for simple identifications or require that a basic calculation be made based on the chart.

The answer is C.

67. A building in a temperate climate will have some areas that require cooling and others that require heating at the same time. To minimize energy use, the best devices to employ are

    A. energy recovery ventilators
    B. heat pipes
    C. recuperative fuel economizers
    D. water-loop heat pumps

Solution

Water-loop heat pumps use a continuous flow of temperate water to extract heat from areas that need to be cooled and add heat to other areas requiring heating using very little, if any, additional energy input.

Energy recovery ventilators work best in climates where the difference between indoor and outdoor air temperature is high. *Heat pipes* are not appropriate for this use because they would simply pre-warm cool outdoor air. A *recuperative fuel economizer* is another type of system that simply uses hot exhaust gas to preheat incoming air or water. This type of equipment would save energy by increasing the efficiency of the heating plant but would not be as effective as the water-loop heat pump system.

The answer is D.

68. A seven-story office building is to have a variable air volume system. The building will have 105,000 ft² (9750 m²) of net space and an estimated 126,000 ft² (11 700 m²) of gross area. About how much space should be the minimum area allowed for HVAC systems?

    A. 2500 ft² (230 m²)
    B. 3800 ft² (350 m²)
    C. 6300 ft² (580 m²)
    D. 7600 ft² (700 m²)

Solution

For most midsize buildings, an all-air or air-water system needs about 3% to 9% of the gross area for HVAC system mechanical space. Office buildings fall somewhere near the midpoint of the range, so use 6% for this question. 6% of the estimated 126,000 ft² (11 706 m²) gross area is 7560 ft² (702 m²). This is rounded up to 7600 ft² (down to 700 m²), so D is correct as a minimum estimated area.

The answer is D.

69. Select the INCORRECT statement.

    A. A health center would probably use no. 4 or no. 5 fuel oil.
    B. Heat pumps rely on solar energy more than on electricity.
    C. Natural gas has a higher heating value than does propane.
    D. Electricity is not a good choice for powering boilers in remote areas.

Solution

Propane has a heating value of 2500 Btu/ft³ (93.1 MJ/m³), whereas natural gas has a heating value of 1050 Btu/ft³ (39.1 MJ/m³).

The answer is C.

70. A main trunk duct is to be placed in the interstitial space above a suspended ceiling and below the structural framing. The space is not constricted. Assuming equal capacities, which of the following shapes of ducts would be best to use?

    A. rectangular, with the long dimension horizontal
    B. rectangular, with the long dimension vertical
    C. square
    D. round

Solution

A round duct is the most efficient choice and offers the smallest possible perimeter for the same cross-sectional area, thus minimizing friction and pressure loss. A square shape would use the available space most efficiently, but a duct of this shape is not as efficient overall as a round duct. As ducts become more rectangular, they become less efficient and have increased friction loss. A rectangular duct with the long dimension horizontal would only be used if space was a problem.

The answer is D.

71. A standard gas furnace has all the following EXCEPT

    A. a flue
    B. a damper
    C. a combustion chamber
    D. filters

Solution

A standard gas furnace does not have a damper. Only a special energy-saving furnace would sometimes have a damper that automatically closes when the furnace is off.

The answer is B.

72. The heat gain for a building has been calculated at 108,000 Btu/hr (27 216 kcal/hr). A compressive refrigeration machine of _____ tons (_____ metric tons) should be specified. (Fill in the blank.)

Solution

A ton of air conditioning is equivalent to 12,000 Btu/hr (3024 kcal/hr). Dividing 108,000 Btu/hr by 12,000 Btu/hr (27 216 kcal/hr by 3024 kcal/hr) gives 9 tons.

> *Study Note*: Modern refrigeration has its roots in the ice-making industry. 12,000 Btu/hr (3024 kcal/hr) is the amount of refrigeration needed to make one ton of ice per day from 32°F (0°C) water.

The answer is 9 tons.

73. An economizer cycle

    A. cools only as much chilled water as required by the demand load
    B. uses outdoor air to cool a building
    C. automatically reduces the amount of time the compressor runs
    D. uses air and water to cool the condenser coils

Solution

An economizer cycle introduces outdoor air when the ambient temperature is low enough to assist in cooling.

The answer is B.

74. Which of the following can produce a change in state?

    A. sensible heat only
    B. latent heat only
    C. sensible and latent heat
    D. none of the above

Solution

Adding latent heat produces a change in state of water and other substances.

The answer is B.

75. Air barriers are designed to stop infiltration and exfiltration caused by all of the following EXCEPT

    A. wind pressure
    B. stack pressure
    C. HVAC fan pressure
    D. vapor pressure

Solution

Wind pressure, stack pressure, and HVAC fan pressure can all influence infiltration and exfiltration rates. Vapor pressure does not cause air movement; rather, vapor pressure is a movement of moisture.

The answer is D.

76. Which of the following strategies would effectively reduce the noise caused by a duct system without reducing airflow?

    A. Specify duct liners for all supply and return ducts.
    B. Specify 90° bends in short duct runs.
    C. Provide an active noise-canceling system emitting out-of-phase noise.
    D. Specify fiberglass baffles.

Solution

An active noise-canceling system would help to reduce the noise in a duct system without reducing airflow. This type of system analyzes the noise from the blowers and other system components and synthesizes a noise that is exactly out of phase with the mechanical noise. The two sounds cancel each other and the result is perceived silence.

The answer is C.

ELECTRICAL

77. Electrical systems in single family homes and duplexes commonly use which type of conductor?

    A. individual wires in EMT
    B. nonmetallic sheathed cable
    C. BX cable
    D. flexible metal-clad cable

Solution

Nonmetallic sheathed cable, also called Romex®, consists of two or more conductors and a ground wire encased in a plastic jacket. This type of unprotected cable is permitted in wood-framed residential buildings and buildings not exceeding three stories as long as it is concealed behind walls and ceilings.

Individual conductors placed in rigid metal conduit, such as *electric metallic tubing* (EMT), intermediate metal conduit (IMC), or rigid steel conduit, are typically used in commercial construction or in hazardous areas. *Flexible metal-clad cable*, or BX, consists of two or more conductors inside a continuous spiral-wound strip of steel cable. This cable is used where metal shielding is required along with the flexibility to remodel or to connect fixtures that may need to be moved.

The answer is B.

78. The electrical symbol shown represents a

    A. triple-position switch
    B. junction box holding three switches
    C. switch for a light controlled from two locations
    D. switch for a light controlled from three locations

Solution

This is the symbol for a three-way switch. This type of switch controls a light from two different switches in different locations.

The "3" in the symbol indicates the number of conductors (not including the ground wire) that make the switch work. A "4" subscript would indicate a four-way switch, or one that can control the same light from three different locations.

The answer is C.

79. In a simple alternating-current circuit serving incandescent lamps, the amperage in the circuit is calculated by

    A. multiplying the impedance by the circuit voltage
    B. multiplying the power factor by the total wattage
    C. dividing the circuit voltage by the total wattage
    D. dividing the total wattage by the circuit voltage

Solution

Power in alternating-current circuits is calculated using the following formula.

$$W = VI(\text{PF})$$

The formula can also be expressed as

$$I = \frac{W}{V(\text{PF})}$$

In the given formulas, the following nomenclature applies.

I	current in amps
PF	power factor
V	voltage of the circuit
W	power in watts

For circuits with resistive loads, such as incandescent lights, the power factor is equal to 1, so the calculation is the total wattage divided by the circuit voltage.

> *Study Note:* Review the differences between direct-current (DC) circuits and alternating-current (AC) circuits. In DC circuits, current is directly proportional to voltage, *V*, and inversely proportional to resistance, *R*. In AC circuits, resistance is known as impedance, which is comprised of resistance and reactance and causes a phase change difference between voltage and current. This is known as the power factor (PF).

The answer is D.

80. A power distribution system is to be specified for an open office area. Which of the following is the most flexible and economical alternative?

    A. access floor system
    B. underfloor raceway system
    C. cellular metal floor raceways
    D. ceiling raceway system with pole raceways

Solution

Any of the options would allow flexibility, but the *ceiling raceway system with pole raceways* would be the least expensive.

An *access floor system* consists of individual panels, typically 24 in (610) square, supported on adjustable pedestals above the structural floor. These systems provide unlimited flexibility for routing power, communications, and air supply, but are expensive and not justified unless a great deal of cabling is involved or future changes will be extensive (such as in a computer room.) An *underfloor raceway system* consists of a series of parallel rectangular metal raceways laid on the structural slab and covered with concrete. A *cellular metal floor raceway* is similar in concept, but is part of the structure. Raceways are similar to standard metal decking and serve as conduits for power and communication cabling. In both underfloor and cellular metal floor systems, the raceways are tapped when power and communication outlets are required.

The answer is D.

81.   Electrical operating costs in a single-tenant commercial building can be minimized by using which of the following techniques?

I.   daylighting
II.   indirect lighting
III. load control
IV.   multiple metering

    A.   I and III only
    B.   II and III only
    C.   I, III, and IV only
    D.   II, III, and IV only

Solution

Daylighting can be used to reduce electrical lighting requirements. *Load control* is a way of avoiding peak-demand electrical charges by automatically or manually shutting off nonessential electrical loads before the peak demand is reached.

Indirect lighting alone would probably not reduce power use; in fact, it may even increase power use because more wattage might be needed to achieve the required lighting level than would be needed with direct or task lighting. *Multiple metering* is only used for multi-tenant spaces and would not result in an overall cost savings for a commercial building.

The answer is A.

82.   Codes limit the number of conductors permitted in a conduit for which two of the following reasons?

I.   to maintain maximum ampacity
II.   to control heat buildup in the conduit
III. to minimize problems with harmonic currents
IV.   to prevent damage to the conductors when they are pulled through the conduit

    A.   I and III
    B.   II and III
    C.   II and IV
    D.   III and IV

Solution

Too many conductors carrying too much current in an enclosed area can generate excessive heat. In addition, conductors can be damaged if too many are pulled through a small conduit. For these reasons, the National Electrical Code (NEC) limits the number of conductors permitted in a conduit.

The NEC only requires that the ampacity (the current-carrying capacity) of conductors be derated if the number of conductors in a raceway or conduit exceeds three (not counting the neutral conductor). Harmonic currents are only a problem with unconventional electrical loads such as computers, electronic lighting ballasts, and other electronic equipment. When these types of loads are supplied by conductors, the neutral conductor must be counted as one of the three allowable conductors in a conduit before ampacity must be derated.

The answer is C.

83.   Which of the following is NOT a type of photovoltaic cell?

    A.   crystalline
    B.   polycrystalline
    C.   thin-film
    D.   transparent

Solution

There is no such thing as a transparent photovoltaic cell.

The answer is D.

84.   Which of the following precautions should be taken if aluminum conductors are used in a building?

I.   Leads should be cleaned prior to making connections.
II.   Special conduit should be specified.
III. Licensed electricians should be required to perform the installation.
IV.   All joints should be soldered.
V.   Larger sizes will be needed than if copper conductors were used.

    A.   III and V only
    B.   I, II, and III only
    C.   I, III, and V only
    D.   II, III, and V only

Solution

Because of the potential for oxidation, the leads of aluminum conductors must be cleaned prior to installation. The special requirements of aluminum conductors and the danger of incorrect installation make it necessary that a licensed electrician do the work. Aluminum conductors must be larger than copper conductors to carry the same amperage.

The answer is C.

85.   High voltages are used in commercial buildings because

    A.   conductors and conduit can be smaller
    B.   a wider variety of loads can be accommodated
    C.   commercial buildings require more power
    D.   transformers can step down the voltages to whatever is required

Solution

As voltages increase, current may be decreased and the system will still provide the same amount of power. Lower currents require smaller conductors. For large commercial buildings, smaller conductors translate to less expense in conductors and conduit, as well as easier installation of smaller wires.

The answer is A.

86.   Which would be the best location for a transformer for a large school building?

    A.   on the power pole serving the building
    B.   in a separate room near the exterior wall
    C.   outside, on a transformer pad close to the main switchgear
    D.   in a protective shed where power from the utility company enters the property

Solution

A transformer vault near the exterior wall would be the best choice for protection, ventilation, and ease of installation and removal. A large school building would require high voltage service from the utility company and step-down transformers provided by the owner. This type of transformer could not be installed on a pole. Although the transformer could be placed on a pad outside the building, this would leave it exposed to possible vandalism and might present a danger to the students.

The answer is B.

87.   Electrical equipment and fixtures should meet the standards of which testing agency?

    A.   UL
    B.   ASTM
    C.   NEC
    D.   IBEW

Solution

Underwriters Laboratories (UL) is an independent testing agency that verifies that equipment sold in the United States and other countries meets their published minimum standards of safety. The *National Electrical Code* (NEC) or a similar code in effect in a jurisdiction will often specify that electrical system components be "UL Listed." This means that the product *as a whole* was tested in the laboratory. The UL symbol (the letters UL with a circle around them) is applied to the exterior of the product along with the word LISTED, a code number, and the product name.

ASTM, originally known as the American Society for Testing and Materials but now known as ASTM International, is an organization that develops technical standards for materials, products, systems, and services. IBEW is the International Brotherhood of Electrical Workers, a labor union representing those who work in the electrical and related industries.

The answer is A.

88. The simultaneous production of electricity and heat from a single fuel source is known as which of the following?

    A. combustion
    B. cogeneration
    C. distributed generation
    D. transmission

Solution

Cogeneration allows heat and electricity to be produced at the same time from one fuel source. Either heat or electricity is considered "free energy" because it is a by-product of producing the other. As a fossil fuel is converted to heat, then to steam, then to mechanical energy, and then to electrical energy, a vast amount of heat is produced. Cogeneration captures this heat and uses it for heating a building or for hot water heating.

The answer is B.

LIGHTING

89. A footlambert (candela per square meter) is the unit of

    A. candlepower
    B. illuminance
    C. luminance
    D. luminous intensity

Solution

Luminance is the luminous flux per unit of projected area and unit solid angle leaving a surface, either reflected or transmitted, and is expressed in footlamberts (candelas per square meter). Luminance takes into account the reflectance and transmittance properties of materials and the directions from which they are viewed. Luminance is sometimes mistakenly called brightness. Luminance is calculated by multiplying the reflectance of material times the illuminance (measured in footcandles or lux).

The answer is C.

90. Which of the following types of lamps provides the best color rendition of skin tones?

    A. cool-white fluorescent
    B. incandescent
    C. mercury vapor
    D. metal halide

Solution

An incandescent lamp has a high color rendering index (CRI) and low color temperature, with a predominance of light in the red range. These characteristics give a complimentary rendering to skin tones.

A cool white fluorescent lamp has more blue and green light in its spectral distribution and makes skin tones appear more gray and washed out. Both mercury vapor and metal halide lamps have poor color rendering indexes and are not appropriate for lighting areas where skin tone rendition is important.

The answer is B.

91. The zonal cavity method of calculating average illumination on the work surface for a given number of luminaires depends on which of the following variables? (Choose the four that apply.)

    A. angle of light
    B. dirt accumulation
    C. efficacy of the lamp
    D. lumens per lamp
    E. room size
    F. wall reflectance

Solution

The *zonal cavity method* is used to calculate the total number of luminaires required to achieve the desired average illumination on the work surface, which is assumed to be 30 in (760) above the floor. The variables considered in the calculation include the level of illumination desired, the area of the room, the number of lamps in each luminaire, the lumen output of each lamp, the coefficient of utilization, the light loss factor, wall reflectance, and the gradual loss of light due to dirt accumulation.

The *coefficient of utilization* (CU) is a measure of the efficiency of a particular luminaire in outputting light and is based on the design of the luminaire itself, the reflectance of the room, and the size of the room. The *light loss factor* represents a degradation of ideal light output due to aging of the lamp and gradual dirt accumulation on the lamp.

The answer is B, D, E, and F.

92. Problems with veiling reflections in a general-purpose workroom could best be reduced by

    A. substituting ambient light for direct light fixtures
    B. repositioning the light fixtures
    C. reducing the brightness of the light fixtures
    D. changing the type of lamps

Solution

A *veiling reflection* is glare caused when the image of a light source is reflected from a viewing surface into the eye. The best way to reduce it is to provide general background illumination (ambient lighting) so the light sources are not concentrated in the area of the lamp.

Repositioning the luminaires (or the task) can reduce veiling reflections, but only when the task is in a specific location in relation to the light source. In a general-purpose workroom this would not be feasible. Reducing the brightness of the light source would help, but would also reduce the illumination provided for the task. Changing the type of lamps would have little effect on reflected glare.

The answer is A.

93. Variables that must be considered when designing for daylighting include all of the following EXCEPT

    A. glass transmittance
    B. height of the head of the glass
    C. longitude of the site
    D. outdoor surface reflection

Solution

The longitude of the site is not a factor in daylighting design. The latitude of the site might have a minor influence on how a daylighting design is implemented, but this is not a critical variable.

Variables that affect daylighting include the brightness of the sky (which is affected by solar altitude, cloud conditions, and time of day), the area of the glass, the height of the head of the glass, the transmittance of the glass, the reflectance of surfaces within the rooms and nearby outdoor surfaces, and obstructions such as overhangs and trees.

The answer is C.

94. For a room with a standard window whose head is 8 ft (3 m) above the floor, daylighting could be used for illumination for a distance from the window of approximately

    A. 8 ft (3 m)
    B. 12 ft (4.5 m)
    C. 16 ft (6 m)
    D. 20 ft (7.5 m)

Solution

For a window with no light shelf, daylighting is effective for a distance of about 1.5 times the head height of the window. With a light shelf, the effective distance increases to about 2.0 to 2.5 times the head height.

$$(8 \text{ ft})(1.5) = 12 \text{ ft}$$

$$(3 \text{ m})(1.5) = 4.5 \text{ m}$$

The answer is B.

95. What combination of lighting would be the most appropriate choice for a women's clothing store?

    A. color-improved mercury lamps with metal halide accent lighting
    B. limited natural daylight, warm white deluxe fluorescent for general illumination, and tungsten halogen for accent lighting
    C. incandescent general lighting with low-voltage accent lighting on displays
    D. daylighting for general illumination and incandescent fixtures for dressing areas and display lighting

Solution

The combination of limited natural light, warm white fluorescent general illumination, and tungsten halogen accent lighting offers the best balance of appropriate color rendering and energy efficiency. Daylighting would provide natural light for viewing clothes and excellent color rendering, but would need to be limited in order to prevent damage to delicate fabrics. Warm white deluxe lamps would be energy efficient and provide a pleasant, overall light. The tungsten halogen accent lights will provide sparkle to jewelry displays and highlight featured merchandise.

Mercury lamps and metal halide lighting have cooler tones which may render colors inappropriately. Incandescent fixtures throughout would not be energy efficient. Using daylighting for general illumination could damage fabrics and would limit the store's hours of operation to daylight hours.

The answer is B.

96. Which three of the following would an architect be most concerned about when designing the lighting for an office space with computer workstations and standard desks?

I.   color rendering index
II. visual comfort probability
III. veiling reflection
IV. reflected glare
V.   task/surrounds brightness ratio

    A.   I, II, and III
    B.   I, III, and V
    C.   II, III, and IV
    D.   III, IV, and V

Solution

In an office space where computer monitors and standard office tasks are present, the architect should be concerned with two results of glare. *Veiling reflection* would be of concern for standard office tasks such as writing and reading, whereas *reflected glare* would be critical in using the monitors. The *brightness ratios* between the tasks and their surroundings are important, especially when employees spend hours in front of a computer monitor. The *color rendering index* and *visual comfort probability* are less important.

The answer is D.

97. An architect wants to increase the expected lighting level of a room. Which of the following steps could accomplish this?

    A.   Change to a lamp type with a lower efficiency.
    B.   Suggest to the owner that the lamps be replaced infrequently.
    C.   Use finishes with a lower light reflectance value.
    D.   Change to luminaires with a higher coefficient of utilization.

Solution

Luminaires with a higher *coefficient of utilization* (CU) allow more light from the lamps to reach the desired surfaces. Lamps with a higher efficency (not lower) should be selected, although the selection of this type of fixture would have to be balanced against the change in color temperature. Lumen output decreases as lamps age and as dirt accumulates on them. Changing lamps often would help maintain the initial footcandle level. Room finishes with high light reflectance values can make a significant increase in the total light level in a room.

The answer is D.

98. A spotlight shining perpendicularly to a wall 15 ft (5 m) away has a candlepower output of 3500 cd. The wall finish is paint, with a reflectance of 75%. What is the luminance of the wall at the point where the wall is perpendicular to the direction of light?

    A.   4.90 fL (44.0 cd/m²)
    B.   11.7 fL (105 cd/m²)
    C.   15.6 fc (140 lx)
    D.   55.7 fc (500 lx)

Solution

In this problem, the footcandle (lux) level of the light shining on the wall must first be determined. Because the direction of light is perpendicular to the wall, the inverse square law is used.

In U.S. units:

$$E = \frac{I}{d^2}$$
$$= \frac{3500 \text{ cd}}{(15 \text{ ft})^2}$$
$$= 15.56 \text{ fc}$$

In SI units:

$$E = \frac{I}{d^2}$$
$$= \frac{3500 \text{ cd}}{(5 \text{ m})^2}$$
$$= 140 \text{ lx}$$

Once the footcandle (lx) level is determined, it is multiplied by the reflectance to find the brightness. Reflectance is the ratio of reflected light to incident light. The former is measured in footlamberts (U.S. units) or candelas per square meter (SI units), the latter in footcandles (U.S.) or lux (SI).

In U.S. units:

$$(15.56 \text{ fc})(0.75) = 11.7 \text{ fL}$$

In SI units:

$$(140 \text{ lx})(0.75) = 105 \text{ cd/m}^2$$

The answer is B.

99. Glass that changes darkness in response to a change in the level of daylight is

    A. chromogenic
    B. electrochromic
    C. photochromic
    D. thermochromic

Solution

Glass that changes darkness in response to a change in the level of daylight is *photochromic*. This type of material is most commonly used for eyeglasses, but also has applications within the building industry.

The answer is C.

100. Which of the following units would be used to measure the brightness of daylight coming through a window?

    A. footcandle
    B. candela
    C. footlambert
    D. candlepower

Solution

Footlambert is the unit of measure of the brightness (or luminance) of a surface and takes into account the transmittance properties of the glass. *Footcandle* is the unit of measure of the light incident on a transmitting or reflecting surface. *Candela* is the SI unit for *candlepower*, which is a measure of luminous intensity.

The answer is C.

101. Why would high-pressure sodium lamps be favored over low-pressure sodium lamps in a storage warehouse?

    A. They are less expensive.
    B. They have a longer lamp life.
    C. They can operate at higher, more efficient voltages.
    D. They have better color-rendering properties.

Solution

Low-pressure sodium lamps produce a monochromatic yellow light that would not be appropriate in a storage warehouse where people may have to discriminate between colors.

The answer is D.

102. An architect is designing an art school at a major university. Which combination of daylighting and electric lighting would be the most appropriate choice for the painting studios?

    A. south-facing windows and incandescent recessed lights
    B. north-facing windows and skylights and fixtures with high-CRI fluorescent lamps
    C. windows to the east and west and fluorescent fixtures in coves at the perimeter of the studio
    D. north-facing skylights and metal halide lamps at each workstation

Solution

Art studios require optimal color rendering and even daylight. The best combination of natural and artificial lighting techniques would be north-facing windows and skylights along with the best quality high-color rendering index lamps that the budget will allow. Task lighting should also be provided for the students' work areas.

The answer is B.

103. Adding white to a color pigment results in a

    A. shade
    B. tint
    C. hue
    D. chroma

Solution

Adding white to a color pigment makes it lighter and the result is called a *tint*; adding black makes it darker and the result is called a *shade*. *Value* is a characteristic of a pigment that describes its lightness or darkness. *Hue* defines a color—red, blue, yellow, and so on. *Chroma* defines a color's saturation.

The answer is B.

ACOUSTICS

104. Two adjacent rooms separated by an acoustical partition are shown. There is a noise-producing source in room B.

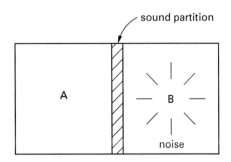

The noise reduction in room A is dependent on all of the following EXCEPT the

- A. area of the partition
- B. thickness of the partition
- C. transmission loss of the partition
- D. absorption of surfaces in room A

Solution

The thickness of a partition or other acoustical separation is irrelevant to the total noise reduction within a space. Factors which would influence the effectiveness of the partition are transmission loss, the area of the barrier, and the total sound absorption within the "quiet" space.

> *Study Note:* Understand the difference between transmission loss and noise reduction. *Transmission loss* (TL) is the difference (in decibels) between the sound power incident on a barrier in a source room and the sound power radiated into a receiving room on the opposite side of the barrier. It is typically a laboratory measurement. *Noise reduction* (NR) is the arithmetic difference (in decibels) between the intensity levels in two rooms separated by a barrier having a given transmission loss level.

The formula for calculating the noise reduction is

$$\text{NR} = \text{TL} + 10 \log \frac{A}{S}$$

A total acoustical absorption of the receiving room, in sabins (ft²)(sabins (m²))
NR   noise reduction, in decibels (dB)
S area of the barrier, in ft² (m²)
TL   transmission loss level of the barrier, in decibels (dB)

The answer is B.

105. An existing partition separating two rooms is felt to be insufficient for reducing sound transmission. The partition consists of 4 in (100) metal studs spaced 24 in (600) on center with a single layer of ⁵⁄₈ in (16) gypsum board on each side. There are no penetrations in the partition. To improve the transmission loss of the partition in the most economical way, which of the following modifications should the architect recommend?

- A. Add resilient channels to one side of the wall and attach a single layer of gypsum board to the channels. Glue an additional layer of gypsum board to the other side.
- B. Add sound-absorbing panels to the noisy side of the partition, and add an additional layer of gypsum board to the opposite side.
- C. Remove one layer of gypsum board, install sound-attenuating insulation, and replace the wall finish with a sound-deadening board and a finish layer of gypsum board.
- D. Cover one side of the partition with an additional layer of gypsum board, and add two additional layers of gypsum board to the other side.

Solution

The best way of improving the transmission loss would be to add mass and resiliency to the partition. This can be accomplished economically by adding extra gypsum board and mounting one layer on resilient channels.

Sound-absorbing panels would not affect the transmission loss; they would only affect the noise reduction in the room on the side where the panels were installed. Removing the wall finish would not be the most economical method for the results obtained by adding insulation and then replacing new wallboard over sound-deadening board. Adding the extra mass of three layers of gypsum board would not be as effective as using resilient channels with two additional layers of gypsum board as in option A.

The answer is A.

106. In order for their benefits to be clearly noticeable, changes to a partition assembly must reduce the sound transmission by

- A. 1 dB
- B. 3 dB
- C. 5 dB
- D. 10 dB

Solution

Although the sensation of loudness is subjective, changes of 5 dB are clearly noticeable.

Changes in apparent loudness of 1 dB are almost imperceptible. Changes of 3 dB are just barely perceptible. Changes of 10 dB are perceived as twice or half as loud.

The answer is C.

107. The partition assembly shown would be best for controlling which of the following kinds of acoustic situations? (Choose the two that apply.)

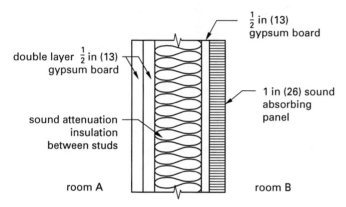

A. impact noise
B. excessive reverberation in room A
C. excessive reverberation in room B
D. transmission from room A to room B
E. transmission from room B to room A
F. mechanical vibration

Solution

The sound absorbing panel in room B would help control excessive reverberation in this space. The hard surface on the room A side of the partition would not control excess reverberation in room A. The double layer of gypsum board would help improve the transmission loss of the wall. Because noise reduction between two spaces is dependent on the transmission loss of the wall, the area of the wall, and the absorption of the surfaces in the receiving room, this assembly would do a better job of reducing sound transmission from room A to room B (because the absorptive panel is in room B) than from room B to room A. The partition would do little to control impact noise or mechanical vibration.

The answer is C and D.

108. A copy machine in an office workroom has a sound intensity level of 65 dB. A computer printer with a sound intensity level of 69 dB is added to the space. What will be the resulting sound intensity level?

A. 69 dB
B. 71 dB
C. 73 dB
D. 134 dB

Solution

Decibel levels are added logarithmically, not arithmatically. To express their combined effect, first determine the difference in sound intensity levels between the two sound sources. Then use the table shown to add the appropriate factor to the larger dB level.

difference in dB level	add to the larger dB level
0	3.0
1	2.5
2	2.1
3	1.8
4	1.5
5	1.2
6	1.0
7	0.8
8	0.6
9	0.5
10	0.4

$$69 \text{ dB} - 65 \text{ dB} = 4 \text{ dB}$$
$$69 \text{ dB} + 1.5 \text{ dB} = 70.5 \text{ dB} \quad (71 \text{ dB})$$

The answer is B.

109. What is the single number often used to evaluate the acoustic qualities of partitions?

A. noise reduction coefficient
B. sound absorption coefficient
C. noise insulation class
D. sound transmission class

Solution

The *sound transmission class* (STC) gives the designer a quick way to evaluate a variety of types of tested partitions in the common frequency ranges.

The answer is D.

110. Which of the following statements are FALSE? (Choose the two that apply.)

A. Sensitivity to sound varies between sexes.

B. People are generally more sensitive to middle and high frequencies than to low frequencies for sounds of equal energy.

C. Most healthy young people can hear sounds in the range of 15 Hz to 25,000 Hz.

D. Practically all common sounds are made up of energy in a wide range of frequencies.

E. Speech is composed of frequencies in the range of 125 Hz to 8000 Hz.

F. Sensitivity to sound varies according to age.

Solution

Sensitivity to sound is not dependent on gender. The low end of sensitivity to sound is somewhere between 20 Hz and 30 Hz, but 15 Hz is too low to be heard, and the generally accepted upper limit is about 20,000 Hz, so 25,000 Hz would be too high to be heard.

The answer is A and C.

111. Which of the following expresses the maximum allowable intensity of background sounds?

A. noise reduction coefficient
B. noise criteria curve
C. sound intensity
D. inverse square law

Solution

Noise criteria curves are used to specify the allowable sound pressure levels at octave band center frequencies.

The answer is B.

112. Which of these factors affects reverberation time?

A. decibel level
B. frequency
C. room volume
D. sound intensity

Solution

A room's *reverberation time* is defined as the time it takes for sound to decay by 60 dB. Reverberation time is dependent on total room absorption and room volume. It is not affected by the sound's decibel level, frequency, or intensity.

The answer is C.

113. A room 15 ft (4.6 m) wide by 20 ft (6.1 m) long by $8^1/_2$ ft (2.6 m) high is finished with the following materials of listed absorptions.

	NRC	125	250	500	1000	2000	4000
floor, wood	0.10	0.15	0.11	0.10	0.07	0.06	0.07
walls, gypsum board	0.05	0.10	0.08	0.05	0.03	0.03	0.03
ceiling, acoustical tile	0.60	0.29	0.29	0.55	0.75	0.73	0.57
window, glass	0.15	0.35	0.25	0.18	0.12	0.07	0.04

On one wall there is a window $3^1/_2$ ft (1.1 m) high by 8 ft (2.4 m) long. What is the total absorption of the room?

A. 228 sabins (ft²)   (21.2 sabins (m²))
B. 242 sabins (ft²)   (22.9 sabins (m²))
C. 266 sabins (ft²)   (24.7 sabins (m²))
D. 282 sabins (ft²)   (26.2 sabins (m²))

Solution

To find the total absorption when calculation at specific frequencies is not required, the NRC, or noise reduction coefficient, is used. The total absorption is the summation of all the individual absorptions according to the formula $A = \Sigma Sa$.

In U.S. units:

floor: (15 ft)(20 ft)(0.10 sabins/ft²) = 30 sabins
walls: ((15 ft + 15 ft + 20 ft + 20 ft)
        × (8.5 ft) − (3.5 ft)(8 ft))
        × (0.05 sabins/ft²)   = 28 sabins
window: (3.5 ft)(8 ft)(0.15 sabins/ft²) = 4 sabins
ceiling: (15 ft)(20 ft)(0.60 sabins/ft²) = 180 sabins
total   242 sabins

In SI units:

floor: (4.6 m)(6.1 m)(0.10 sabins/m²) = 2.8 sabins
walls: ((4.6 m + 4.6 m + 6.1 m + 6.1 m)
        × (2.6 m) − (1.1 m)(2.4 m))
        × (0.05 sabins/m²)   = 2.7 sabins
window: (1.1 m)(2.4 m)(0.15 sabins/m²) = 0.4 sabins
ceiling: (4.6 m)(6.1 m)(0.60 sabins/m²) = 17 sabins
total   22.9 sabins

The answer is B.

114. During a design development presentation to the building committee of a middle school, one of the teachers expresses concern that there might be a noise problem between the classrooms shown in the partial plan. The larger classroom will be used for open discussions, movies, lab work, and other loud activities while the smaller space will be used primarily for individual study. Both classrooms are scheduled to have gypsum board partitions, vinyl tile floors, and suspended acoustical ceilings.

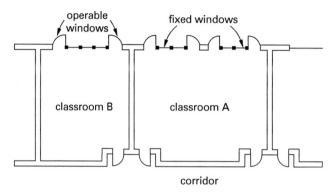

Rank the following possible design modifications, placing the most effective and economical suggestion first.

I.   Substitute carpeting for tile in both rooms.

II. Move the operable windows nearest the separating wall so that they are further from it, and change the direction of their swings.

III. Reroute the ductwork and conduit penetrations so that they pass through the separating wall above the suspended ceiling, and write specifications to direct that any remaining penetrations be tightly sealed.

IV. Replan the layout so that there is a small audiovisual storage room between the classrooms.

V.   Add an extra layer of gypsum board to each side of the separating partition, and specify that the cavity be filled with sound-attenuating insulation.

VI. Hire an acoustical consultant to determine the special frequency problems associated with the activities planned for the larger classroom, and design custom sound-absorbing surfaces and partitions accordingly.

   A. II, III, V, I, IV, VI
   B. III, II, V, I, VI, IV
   C. IV, II, III, V, VI, I
   D. V, III, II, I, IV, VI

Solution

The simplest, least expensive suggestion during design development would be to reorient the operable windows so sound from one classroom did not reflect off an open window and on to an open window in the adjacent classroom. Also, during design development, it is an easy matter to coordinate routing of mechanical and electrical work to minimize acoustical problems.

Moving the systems above the acoustical ceiling provides an additional layer of absorptive material between the equipment and the occupants. It is also less expensive to seal those penetrations through the partition that are out of sight.

The third priority would be to add the extra layers of gypsum board and sound-attenuating insulation to improve the transmission loss of the partition. For the small additional cost, sound transmission would be greatly reduced. Substituting carpeting for tile would help absorb noise in each room, but would not impact the transmission loss through the wall. The cost of the change to the floor finish would probably be more than the cost of adding the gypsum board and insulation, but would still be reasonable for the benefits obtained.

Even though it would greatly limit sound transmission between the two rooms, and would be easy to do during the early planning stages, it does not make sense to place a storage room between the rooms when the potential acoustical problem can be solved by other means.

Least desirable or economical is hiring an acoustical consultant for only this situation. The expected acoustical challenges are not so unusual that the preceding steps would not sufficiently solve the problem.

The answer is A.

115. Which of the following statements about noise reduction between two rooms is FALSE?

   A. Noise reduction is improved with an increase in the transmission loss of the wall separating the two rooms.

   B. The stiffness of the separating wall has some effect on noise reduction.

   C. To improve noise reduction, place absorptive materials on both sides of the separating wall.

   D. An increase in wall area separating the two rooms is detrimental.

Solution

Placing absorptive materials on both sides of the wall would decrease the noise level in the "noisier" room, but noise reduction between the rooms is affected by the transmission loss, the stiffness (damping qualities), and the area of the separating wall.

The answer is C.

116. A material supplier states that adding a certain product to a wall assembly in a critical acoustical situation will increase the noise reduction (STC rating) between two spaces by 3 dB. What is the most appropriate response?

    A.   Determine the additional cost and then decide whether or not to use the product.

    B.   Thank the supplier for stopping by but explain that the architectural firm probably will not be using the product because that amount of noise reduction does not make it worth the effort or cost.

    C.   Specify the product as long as it does not affect the design or construction cost by more than 5%.

    D.   Inquire whether some modification can be made to the product to increase its rating to 6 dB and say that then the architectural firm might consider it.

Solution

Because a change in intensity level of 3 dB is considered "just perceptible," it would probably be better not to use the material regardless of how low the added cost was. Trying to modify the material to 6 dB would also probably not be worth the trouble. To achieve an STC rating 6 dB higher, it would be better to look at another type of construction assembly instead of trying to make do with a modified material. Option D could be correct if the material was such that simply doubling it rather than modifying it would result in a 6 dB increase.

The answer is B.

SPECIALTIES

117. In a large single-tenant building, a LAN system would most commonly serve

    A.   building automation

    B.   computers

    C.   security

    D.   telephones

Solution

LAN is an acronym for *local area network*, which is a system of individual computers, computer servers, and wired or wireless connections that allows all the users in an individual building or complex of buildings to share data on a nonpublic network.

> *Study Note:* A WAN is a *wide area network*, which is a system that connects computers at widely spaced locations to a private network. The locations can be in different cities or different states. Although both systems are intended for private use, they can be, and commonly are, connected with the internet.

The answer is B.

118. Which of the following devices would best control entry to a secure laboratory?

    A.   card reader

    B.   central station alarm

    C.   photoelectric cell

    D.   ultrasonic detector

Solution

A *card reader* is one type of security device that is used to control access.

Security systems are generally comprised of access controls, notification devices, and intrusion detectors. A *central station alarm* is a method of notification. *Photoelectric cells* and *ultrasonic detectors* are devices used for intrusion detection.

The answer is A.

119. A new 80,000 ft² (8000 m²) office building is projected to cost $10,000,000. Approximately what percentages of the construction budget should be allocated to the building's mechanical and electrical systems costs?

- A. mechanical 5%
  electrical 5%
- B. mechanical 15%
  electrical 5%
- C. mechanical 15%
  electrical 15%
- D. mechanical 25%
  electrical 15%

Solution

For an office building of this size, the total mechanical and electrical costs are in the range of 30% of the total construction budget, about equally divided between the two (15% allocated to each). For smaller office buildings, the total costs are in the range of 20%, also about equally divided.

Study Note: Review general cost guidelines for various common building types such as office, retail, educational, and civic.

The answer is C.

120. The following are methods of providing security to a 3000 ft² (300 m²) jewelry shop in a shopping center. Rank the available options in the most likely order from lowest cost to highest cost over a 5 year period.

I. staffed central guard station at the shop entrance
II. numbered keypads on front doors and storage room doors
III. polycarbonate glazing on all display cases
IV. ultrasonic motion detectors connected to the security service

- A. I, II, IV, then III
- B. II, III, IV, then I
- C. III, II, I, then IV
- D. IV, III, II, then I

Solution

The least expensive option in terms of both initial and long-term costs would be the installation of special locks on the doors. The number of doors would be limited, and simple, numbered keypad locks are relatively inexpensive. Polycarbonate display cases would have only an initial cost for purchase and installation. Ultrasonic motion detectors would

be relatively inexpensive to install, but the monthly fee for subscription to a 24-hour monitoring service would increase the long-term cost of this option. The most expensive option is a central guard station with a dedicated employee.

The answer is B.

121. Which of the following would NOT be appropriate for fire protection in an elementary school?

- A. ionization detector
- B. temperature rise detector
- C. photoelectric detector
- D. none of the above

Solution

A *temperature rise detector* would not give early warning to the occupants. If properly located, either an ionization or photoelectric detector would work. *Ionization detectors* sound an alarm when they sense the products of combustion. *Photoelectric detectors* monitor smoke. Either would sound an alarm before a temperature rise detector.

The answer is B.

122. What is the optimal location for an elevator machine room?

- A. beside the elevator on the lowest level of the building
- B. adjacent to the electrical room
- C. above the hoistway
- D. adjacent to the mechanical room

Solution

Ideally, elevator mechanical rooms should be placed above the hoistway. They must be at least as wide as the elevator shaft and generally need to be more than 12 ft (3.65 m) deeper than the hoistway, but the exact size of the space should be calculated considering the type of elevator specified, the sizes of all the equipment to be housed in the space, and the required servicing clearances.

The answer is C.

123. The pyramidal forms of Manhattan skyscrapers built in the early to mid-1900s were the result of

    A. the influence of European tastes and style on American architecture
    B. a response to zoning laws governing setbacks and height restrictions
    C. an attempt to make buildings safer in case of fire by housing fewer people on the uppermost floors
    D. the structural limitations of iron as a building material

Solution

In 1916, New York City passed a zoning law designed to protect access to light and ventilation for all buildings. Skyscrapers were being built as quickly as possible, and New Yorkers feared that these walls of masonry and steel reaching into the sky would make the street level cold, dark, and cavernous. As buildings rose higher and higher, they were required to comply with more stringent setbacks. In order to build the maximum rentable area on their extremely valuable sites, developers adopted the stepped, wedding cake-like shape.

The answer is B.

MECHANICAL AND ELECTRICAL PLAN VIGNETTE

Directions

Complete the provided reflected ceiling plan for a small office suite shown using the symbols given below the floor plan. The solution must show a ceiling grid for acoustical tile and lighting fixtures and a schematic representation of the HVAC plan including air diffusers, return air grilles, ductwork, and fire dampers. Locate light fixtures to achieve the required light level indicated in the program using the light distribution diagrams provided. The lighting layout should minimize overlighting and underlighting and provide for maximum flexibility for furniture layouts.

Program

Suspended Ceiling System

1. Provide a 2 ft by 4 ft (600 by 1200) grid with lay-in acoustical tiles in all spaces.

2. The ceiling height in all spaces is 9 ft 0 in (2740).

3. Interior partitions terminate 4 in (100) above the finished ceiling. Fire-rated partitions and bearing walls extend to the bottom of the floor deck above.

Lighting System

1. Lighting layouts should provide for efficient, uniform illumination. For all spaces except the reception area, use only recessed fluorescent fixtures to provide uniform light distribution with a light level of approximately 70 fc (700 lux) measured at approximately 2 ft 6 in (760) above the floor.

2. For the reception area, use only recessed incandescent fixtures to provide uniform light distribution with a light level of approximately 70 fc (700 lux) measured at approximately 2 ft 6 in (610) above the floor.

3. In addition to the general lighting required above, provide three accent light fixtures along the west wall of the largest office. To achieve the desired effect, the direct light level should be 70 fc (700 lx) at 5 ft 0 in (1500) above the floor. The fixture specification states that this illumination can be achieved by spacing the fixtures 4 ft 0 in (1200) on center and locating them 1 ft 0 in (300) from the wall.

4. Provide exit signs at all egress doors.

HVAC System

The space is served by supply air and return air risers in the shaft shown on the plan. Supply air is provided through ductwork. Return air grilles are open to the plenum. However, the plenum must be connected to the return air riser with rigid ductwork. The HVAC system should provide for uniform air distribution with an economical duct layout conforming to the following.

1. Provide a minimum of one supply air diffuser and one return air grille in each space. An acceptable distribution pattern includes one supply air diffuser and one return air grille for every 150 ft² (14 m²) of floor area or fraction thereof.

2. Each supply air diffuser must be connected to the rigid supply duct system with flexible ducts. Flexible ducts may not exceed 10 ft (3050) in length. Each diffuser must have a separate flexible duct connecting it to the rigid duct system.

3. Flexible ducts may fit through joist webs.

4. Each air diffuser must have a separate flexible duct connecting it to the rigid duct system.

5. Rigid ducts fit under beams, in spaces between joists, and in a zone that extends 2 ft (600) from the beams and is adjacent to the fire-rated walls separating the space from adjacent tenant spaces. Rigid ducts do not fit through joist webs or between the bottoms of joists and the ceiling except within the 2 ft (600) zone mentioned previously.

6. Duct openings in fire-rated partitions must be protected with fire dampers.

Tips

- Be familiar with the contents of each layer.

- On the actual exam, use the *move, adjust* tool and click anywhere within the grid to shift the cells within the perimeter of the grid rectangle.

- On the actual exam, use the *move, adjust* tool and click on the edge of the grid rectangle to increase or decrease the length or width of the entire grid rectangle.

- On the actual exam, use the *move group* tool and click on any part of the grid to move the entire grid rectangle elsewhere.

- If one element of two overlapping elements cannot be selected, keep clicking without moving the mouse until the desired element is highlighted.

Tools

Useful tools include the following.

- *zoom* tool for laying out the ceiling grid
- *rotate* tool for rotating the ceiling grid
- *sketch measure* tool to check for spacing distances from walls

Target Time: 1 hour

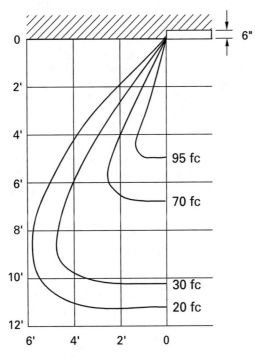

footcandle distribution for recessed
fluorescent fixtures–U.S. units

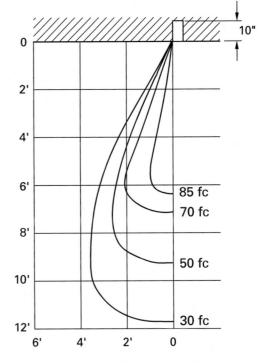

footcandle distribution for recessed
incandescent fixtures–U.S. units

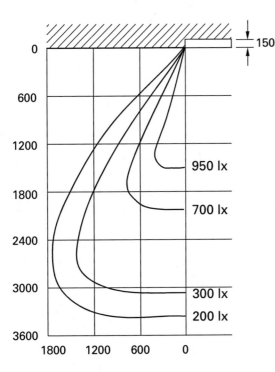

footcandle distribution for recessed
fluorescent fixtures–SI units

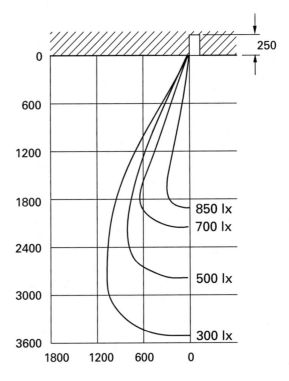

footcandle distribution for recessed
incandescent fixtures–SI units

LIGHT DISTRIBUTION DIAGRAMS

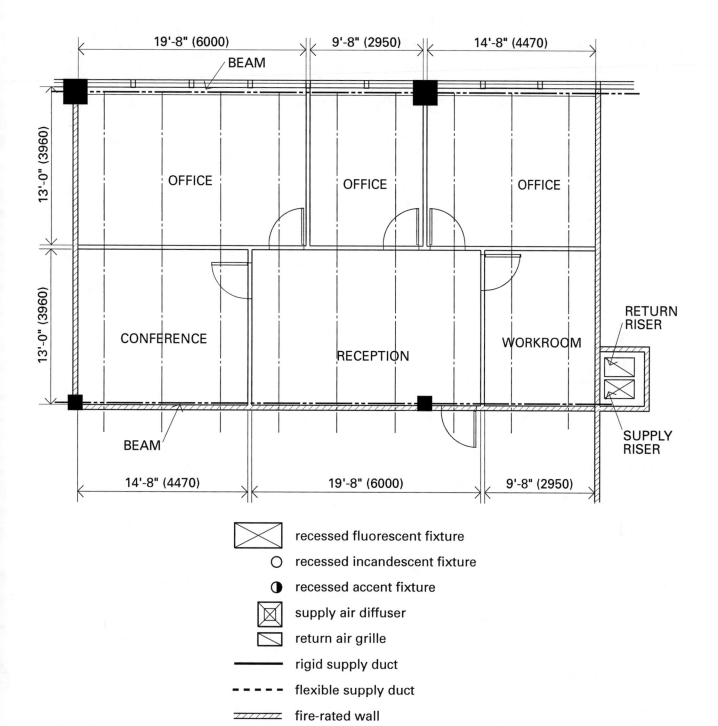

recessed fluorescent fixture

recessed incandescent fixture

recessed accent fixture

supply air diffuser

return air grille

rigid supply duct

flexible supply duct

fire-rated wall

bar joist

beam

fire damper

exit sign

Scale: 1/8" = 1'-0"
[1:100 metric]

MECHANICAL AND ELECTRICAL PLAN:

MECHANICAL AND ELECTRICAL PLAN: SOLVING APPROACH

The first step in completing this vignette is to place the light fixtures. The spacing of the fixtures is dependent on the information given in the light distribution diagrams and the illumination levels stated in the program.

A light distribution diagram depicts the maximum beam spread of a fixture. The x-axis of the diagram indicates the appropriate horizontal spacing between fixtures, and the y-axis indicates the vertical location relative to the ceiling plane. The program will state the desired lighting level and the location at which that level is to be measured. The curves on the diagram indicate the lighting level. For example, in this problem, the desired light level is 70 fc (700 lx) measured at 2 ft 6 in (760) above the floor. The ceiling height is 9 ft 0 in (2740).

In U.S. units:

$$9 \text{ ft } 0 \text{ in} - 2 \text{ ft } 6 \text{ in} = 6 \text{ ft } 6 \text{ in}$$

In SI units:

$$2740 \text{ mm} - 760 \text{ mm} = 1980 \text{ mm}$$

From the diagram, in order to produce a light level of 70 ft (700 lx) at 6 ft 6 in (1980) below the ceiling, the fixtures must be spaced 4 ft (1200) apart. (Maximum beam spread extends 2 ft (600) from the edge of each fixture.) With this information, the lights can be appropriately placed within the rooms. One way to accomplish this is to lay out the fixtures with the proper spacing, then move the lights as a group until they are relatively centered within the space. It may be necessary to move them around a bit until a good location is determined.

The program requires three accent fixtures along the west wall of the largest office. Space the fixtures according to the fixture specification requirements (4 ft 0 in (1200) on center and 1 ft 0 in (300) from the wall) and center the grouping on the accented wall.

Next, lay out the ceiling grid in each room. The light fixture locations will serve as a good guide. Again, it may be necessary to shift things around until the grid fits nicely in the room. The grid should be centered as much as possible, and small pieces of tile at the perimeter of the space should be minimized. Keep in mind that the program states that the interior partitions extend above the ceiling plane; therefore, it is not necessary for the grids in adjacent spaces to align.

With the grid in place, next tackle the layout of the HVAC system. Remember, this is a three-dimensional problem. The program will state the rules for what fits where; the location of rigid ducts is particularly critical. Read the directions carefully. The entire system must be contained within

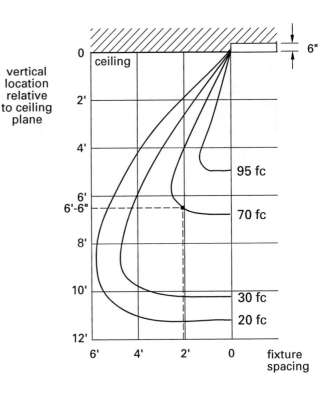

in U.S. units

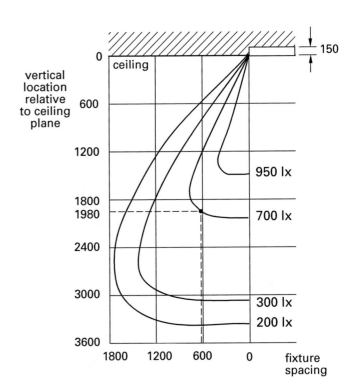

in SI units

the problem area. Do not place anything outside the perimeter walls of the space provided.

It will be necessary to place the rigid supply duct so that the required number of diffusers can be located in each space without exceeding the maximum flexible duct length permitted.

Here are some other considerations when designing the HVAC system.

- The program may state the number of diffusers and returns required in each room, or it may require a specific number of diffusers and returns based on the floor area or a fraction thereof. Make a list of the requirements on your scratch paper, and figure out how many are required in each space, before trying to place them.

- Try to keep diffusers at least 4 ft (1200) from returns.

- Returns may be open to the plenum above or ducted, depending on the vignette's requirements. The program may also call for a specific return to be ducted while others are open to the plenum. Carefully examine the requirements before placing the returns.

- Any time a duct penetrates a fire-rated partition, it must have a fire damper.

- Each diffuser must have its own flexible duct.

- If the program requires the plenum to be connected to the return air riser, show a short run of rigid ductwork. This situation usually requires a fire damper.

Finally, double-check that the solution complies with program requirements; that the proper numbers of diffusers and returns are provided; that duct runs are within acceptable length limits; that exit signs are placed, if required, at egress (outswinging) doors; that required accent lighting is provided; and that the solution is drafted neatly.

MECHANICAL AND ELECTRICAL PLAN: PASSING SOLUTION

All the requirements listed in the program are met with this solution. The grid in each room is centered to provide for uniform illumination, and the rigid duct is located to coordinate with the structure. The light fixtures are properly spaced according to the information given in the light distribution diagrams, and the fixtures are centered in the room. The lengths of flexible duct comply with the program requirements, and fire dampers are placed at all penetrations through fire-rated walls.

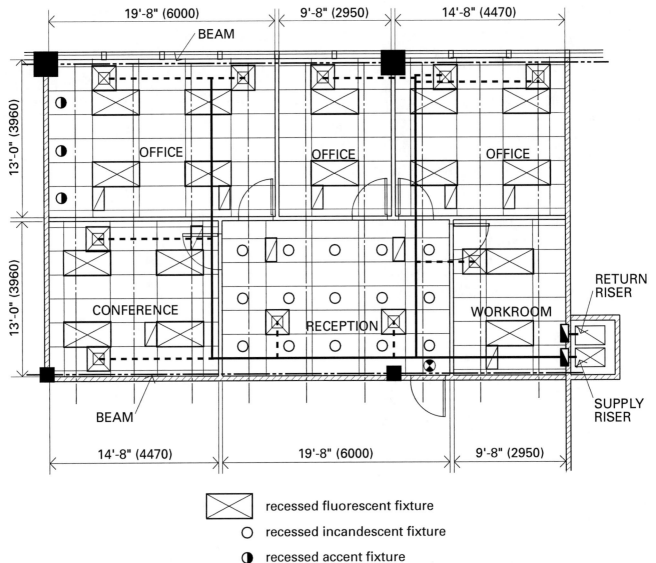

recessed fluorescent fixture

recessed incandescent fixture

recessed accent fixture

supply air diffuser

return air grille

rigid supply duct

flexible supply duct

fire-rated wall

bar joist

beam

fire damper

exit sign

Scale: 1/8" = 1'-0"
[1:100 metric]

**MECHANICAL AND ELECTRICAL PLAN:
PASSING SOLUTION**

MECHANICAL AND ELECTRICAL
PLAN: FAILING SOLUTION

In this solution the length of the rigid duct is excessive, and one of the flexible ducts in the conference room serves two diffusers, which is prohibited by the program. There is only one return air grille in the large office and only one supply diffuser and return air grille in the smaller office in the east portion of the suite. In the large office and the small office there are too many light fixtures (spacing is less than the 4 ft (1200) suggested by the lighting diagrams), and in the reception area there are too few lights. The east-west spacing at 4 ft (1200) is acceptable, but the north-south spacing is too far apart. If the return air riser is shown as a separate element in the shaft, there should be a rigid duct line connecting the fire damper and the return riser. The exit sign and accent lights have been omitted from the solution.

Note 1   Diffuser and return are too close together.

Note 2   Light fixture spacing is incorrect.

Note 3   Return is missing in this space.

Note 4   Two diffusers and two returns are required in this space.

Note 5   Rigid duct is not laid out economically.

Note 6   Small pieces of tile at perimeter of room.

Note 7   Flexible duct serves two diffusers.

Note 8   Light fixture spacing is incorrect.

Note 9   Exit sign is omitted.

Note 10   No connection between plenum and return riser.

Note 11   Accent light fixtures are not shown.

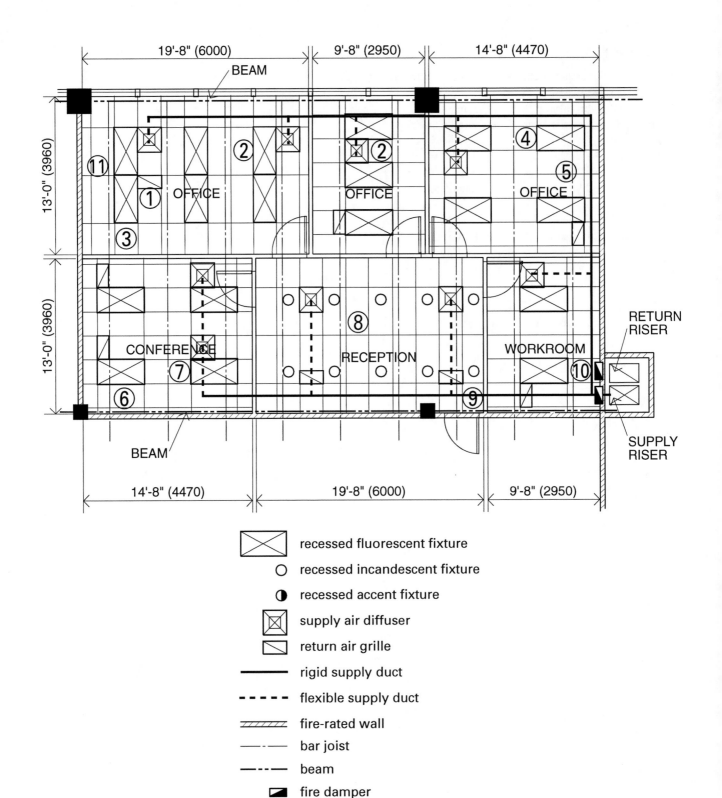

	recessed fluorescent fixture
	recessed incandescent fixture
	recessed accent fixture
	supply air diffuser
	return air grille
	rigid supply duct
	flexible supply duct
	fire-rated wall
	bar joist
	beam
	fire damper
	exit sign

Scale: 1/8" = 1'-0"
[1:100 metric]

MECHANICAL AND ELECTRICAL PLAN:
FAILING SOLUTION

PRACTICE EXAM: MULTIPLE CHOICE

Directions

Reference books should not be used on this practice exam. Besides this book, you should have only a calculator, pencils, and scratch paper. (On the actual exam, these will be provided and should not be brought into the site.)

Target Time: 2 hours

1. Ⓐ Ⓑ Ⓒ Ⓓ
2. Ⓐ Ⓑ Ⓒ Ⓓ
3. Ⓐ Ⓑ Ⓒ Ⓓ
4. Ⓐ Ⓑ Ⓒ Ⓓ
5. _____
6. Ⓐ Ⓑ Ⓒ Ⓓ
7. Ⓐ Ⓑ Ⓒ Ⓓ
8. Ⓐ Ⓑ Ⓒ Ⓓ
9. Ⓐ Ⓑ Ⓒ Ⓓ
10. Ⓐ Ⓑ Ⓒ Ⓓ
11. Ⓐ Ⓑ Ⓒ Ⓓ
12. Ⓐ Ⓑ Ⓒ Ⓓ
13. Ⓐ Ⓑ Ⓒ Ⓓ
14. _____
15. Ⓐ Ⓑ Ⓒ Ⓓ
16. Ⓐ Ⓑ Ⓒ Ⓓ
17. Ⓐ Ⓑ Ⓒ Ⓓ
18. Ⓐ Ⓑ Ⓒ Ⓓ Ⓔ Ⓕ
19. Ⓐ Ⓑ Ⓒ Ⓓ
20. Ⓐ Ⓑ Ⓒ Ⓓ
21. Ⓐ Ⓑ Ⓒ Ⓓ
22. Ⓐ Ⓑ Ⓒ Ⓓ
23. Ⓐ Ⓑ Ⓒ Ⓓ
24. Ⓐ Ⓑ Ⓒ Ⓓ
25. Ⓐ Ⓑ Ⓒ Ⓓ

26. Ⓐ Ⓑ Ⓒ Ⓓ
27. Ⓐ Ⓑ Ⓒ Ⓓ
28. Ⓐ Ⓑ Ⓒ Ⓓ
29. _____
30. Ⓐ Ⓑ Ⓒ Ⓓ
31. Ⓐ Ⓑ Ⓒ Ⓓ
32. Ⓐ Ⓑ Ⓒ Ⓓ
33. Ⓐ Ⓑ Ⓒ Ⓓ
34. Ⓐ Ⓑ Ⓒ Ⓓ
35. Ⓐ Ⓑ Ⓒ Ⓓ
36. Ⓐ Ⓑ Ⓒ Ⓓ
37. Ⓐ Ⓑ Ⓒ Ⓓ
38. Ⓐ Ⓑ Ⓒ Ⓓ
39. Ⓐ Ⓑ Ⓒ Ⓓ
40. Ⓐ Ⓑ Ⓒ Ⓓ
41. Ⓐ Ⓑ Ⓒ Ⓓ Ⓔ Ⓕ
42. Ⓐ Ⓑ Ⓒ Ⓓ
43. Ⓐ Ⓑ Ⓒ Ⓓ Ⓔ Ⓕ
44. Ⓐ Ⓑ Ⓒ Ⓓ
45. Ⓐ Ⓑ Ⓒ Ⓓ
46. Ⓐ Ⓑ Ⓒ Ⓓ
47. Ⓐ Ⓑ Ⓒ Ⓓ
48. Ⓐ Ⓑ Ⓒ Ⓓ
49. Ⓐ Ⓑ Ⓒ Ⓓ
50. Ⓐ Ⓑ Ⓒ Ⓓ Ⓔ Ⓕ

51. Ⓐ Ⓑ Ⓒ Ⓓ
52. Ⓐ Ⓑ Ⓒ Ⓓ
53. Ⓐ Ⓑ Ⓒ Ⓓ
54. Ⓐ Ⓑ Ⓒ Ⓓ
55. Ⓐ Ⓑ Ⓒ Ⓓ
56. Ⓐ Ⓑ Ⓒ Ⓓ Ⓔ Ⓕ
57. Ⓐ Ⓑ Ⓒ Ⓓ
58. Ⓐ Ⓑ Ⓒ Ⓓ
59. Ⓐ Ⓑ Ⓒ Ⓓ
60. Ⓐ Ⓑ Ⓒ Ⓓ
61. Ⓐ Ⓑ Ⓒ Ⓓ
62. _____
63. Ⓐ Ⓑ Ⓒ Ⓓ
64. Ⓐ Ⓑ Ⓒ Ⓓ
65. Ⓐ Ⓑ Ⓒ Ⓓ
66. Ⓐ Ⓑ Ⓒ Ⓓ
67. Ⓐ Ⓑ Ⓒ Ⓓ
68. Ⓐ Ⓑ Ⓒ Ⓓ
69. Ⓐ Ⓑ Ⓒ Ⓓ
70. Ⓐ Ⓑ Ⓒ Ⓓ
71. Ⓐ Ⓑ Ⓒ Ⓓ
72. _____
73. Ⓐ Ⓑ Ⓒ Ⓓ
74. Ⓐ Ⓑ Ⓒ Ⓓ
75. Ⓐ Ⓑ Ⓒ Ⓓ

76. Ⓐ Ⓑ Ⓒ Ⓓ   86. Ⓐ Ⓑ Ⓒ Ⓓ
77. Ⓐ Ⓑ Ⓒ Ⓓ   87. Ⓐ Ⓑ Ⓒ Ⓓ Ⓔ Ⓕ
78. Ⓐ Ⓑ Ⓒ Ⓓ   88. Ⓐ Ⓑ Ⓒ Ⓓ
79. Ⓐ Ⓑ Ⓒ Ⓓ   89. Ⓐ Ⓑ Ⓒ Ⓓ
80. Ⓐ Ⓑ Ⓒ Ⓓ   90. Ⓐ Ⓑ Ⓒ Ⓓ
81. Ⓐ Ⓑ Ⓒ Ⓓ   91. Ⓐ Ⓑ Ⓒ Ⓓ
82. Ⓐ Ⓑ Ⓒ Ⓓ   92. Ⓐ Ⓑ Ⓒ Ⓓ
83. Ⓐ Ⓑ Ⓒ Ⓓ   93. Ⓐ Ⓑ Ⓒ Ⓓ
84. Ⓐ Ⓑ Ⓒ Ⓓ   94. Ⓐ Ⓑ Ⓒ Ⓓ
85. Ⓐ Ⓑ Ⓒ Ⓓ Ⓔ Ⓕ   95. Ⓐ Ⓑ Ⓒ Ⓓ

1.   Which of the following is the most desirable duct shape?

A.

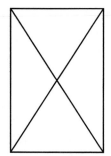

B.

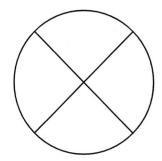

C.

D.

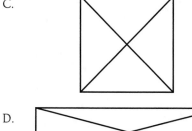

2.   Which of the following building materials has the lowest amount of embodied energy per square foot?

A.   aluminum
B.   ceramic tile
C.   ³/₈ in (9.53) plywood
D.   ¹/₄ in (6.35) tempered glass

3.   Human body temperature is regulated by the

A.   pituitary
B.   thyroid
C.   hypothalamus
D.   skin

4.   Calculate the thermal conductivity (*U*-value) for the wall assembly shown at the section indicated on the plan.

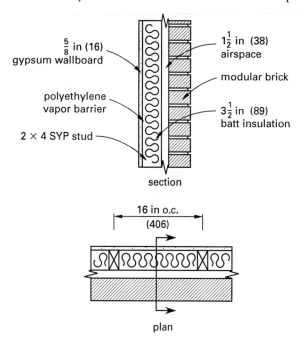

material	R-value (ft²-hr-°F/Btu)	RSI-value (m²·°C/W)
⁵/₈ in (16) gypsum wallboard	0.56	0.10
fiberglass batt insulation	3.3/in	23/m
brick	0.30/in	2.1/m
southern yellow pine stud	1.00/in	6.9/m
plastic film vapor barrier	negligible	negligible
airspace, still air, no reflective surfaces	0.61	0.11
inside air layer, still	0.68	0.12
outside air layer, moving winter air	0.17	0.03

A.   0.068 Btu/ft²-hr-°F (0.38 W/m²·°C)
B.   0.15 Btu/ft²-hr-°F (0.84 W/m²·°C)
C.   0.20 Btu/ft²-hr-°F (1.1 W/m²·°C)
D.   15 Btu/ft²-hr-°F (2.6 W/m²·°C)

5.   An architect is assisting with the renovation of a 1780 farmhouse in Virginia. The total floor area of the farmhouse is approximately 1500 ft² (140 m²). The owner requests a central air conditioning system. The cooling capacity required, rounded to the nearest ton, will be _____ tons. (Fill in the blank.)

6.   Which type of passive solar heating strategy does the following illustration represent?

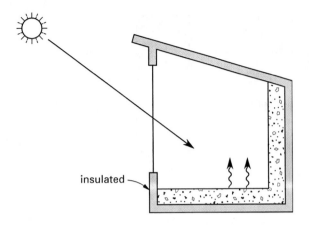

insulated

A.   Trombe wall
B.   sunspace
C.   roof panel
D.   direct gain

7.   Which of the following is NOT used to disinfect water to make it potable?

A.   chlorination
B.   ozonation
C.   ultraviolet light
D.   zeolite process

8.   The goal of a lightning protection system is to

A.   provide a continuous path to the ground for a lightning strike
B.   prevent a lightning strike
C.   prevent damage to computer equipment
D.   attract lightning

9.   An architect is designing a new furniture gallery to be housed within an old bank building. The store will feature modern furniture and artwork and will display approximately one million dollars' worth of inventory. Which of these types of sprinkler systems would be the most appropriate choice for the store?

A.   wet pipe
B.   dry pipe
C.   preaction
D.   deluge

10.   A photoelectric detector will warn of a fire when the fire reaches the

A.   incipient stage
B.   smoldering stage
C.   flame stage
D.   heat stage

11.   Which of the following statements is true?

A.   Smoke detector covers should be used in areas under construction.
B.   Ionization detectors should be installed in a restaurant kitchen.
C.   Smoke detectors may be installed in ductwork in lieu of installation in occupied areas of a building.
D.   Spot heat detectors can detect a fire before any other type of detector.

12.   The sun's seasonal relationship with the earth is described by the

A.   altitude angle
B.   profile angle
C.   azimuth angle
D.   declination angle

13.   According to the Energy Policy Act of 1992, showerheads are required to dispense a maximum of

A.   1.0 gal (3.8 L) of water per minute
B.   1.6 gal (6.1 L) of water per minute
C.   2.5 gal (9.5 L) of water per minute
D.   3.6 gal (13.6 L) of water per minute

14.   A table lamp is placed 5 ft (5 m) from a wall. The wall is coated with paint with a reflectance factor of 0.79. The intensity of the lamp is 2500 cd. The luminance of the wall is _____ cd/ft^2 (cd/m^2). (Fill in the blank.)

15. An architect is selecting lighting for a classroom filled with computer workstations. The candlepower distribution curves for a variety of fixture types are shown as follows. Which candlepower distribution diagram would be most appropriate for this space?

A.

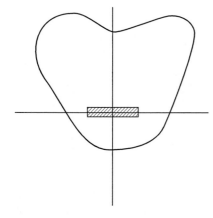

B.

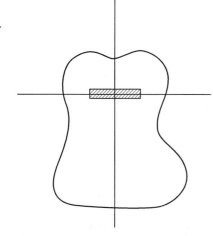

C.

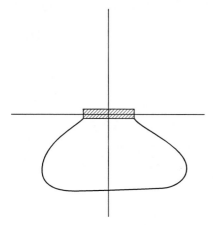

D.

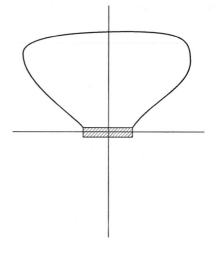

16. The walls of a new coffee shop will be painted a rich pumpkin orange. What type of lighting will provide the best overall color rendering and accent the orange walls?

    A. cool white fluorescent
    B. warm white fluorescent
    C. incandescent
    D. daylight

17. Which type of HID lamp must be installed in a specified burning position?

    A. mercury vapor
    B. metal halide
    C. high-pressure sodium
    D. low-pressure sodium

18. Which of the following statements are true about electronic ballasts installed on fluorescent lamps? (Choose the two that apply.)

    A. Flicker is less than with conventional ballasts.
    B. Lamps cannot start in temperatures below 40°F (4.44°C).
    C. Noise is greater than with conventional ballasts.
    D. Lamps cannot be dimmed.
    E. Existing fixtures with conventional ballasts can be retrofitted with electronic ballasts.
    F. Electronic ballasts are less energy efficient.

19. Which type of lamp typically has the longest life span?

    A. incandescent

    B. fluorescent

    C. metal halide

    D. high-pressure sodium

20. Which type of plastic pipe is suitable for use as a hot water supply line?

    A. CPVC

    B. ABS

    C. PVC

    D. PE

21. An architect is designing an office building for a site in Minnesota. He draws a profile of the site based upon a topographic survey provided by the client. The client asks the architect's opinion on the best location for the building. In order to take advantage of the most favorable microclimate on the site, where should the building be located?

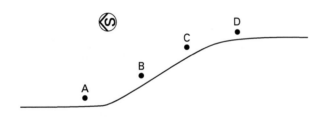

22. What is typically the maximum height building that can utilize an upfeed water supply system?

    A. 20 ft to 30 ft (6 m to 9 m)

    B. 30 ft to 40 ft (9 m to 12 m)

    C. 50 ft to 60 ft (15 m to 18 m)

    D. 70 ft to 80 ft (21 m to 24 m)

23. Which type of pipe is typically used for sanitary lines in nonresidential buildings?

    A. PVC

    B. copper

    C. ABS

    D. cast iron

24. In what type of building would 120/208 voltage, three-phase power be appropriate?

    A. industrial

    B. small commercial

    C. residential

    D. large commercial

25. Where would a sound intensity level of 120 dB be likely to be found?

    A. in a sewing factory

    B. at a rock concert

    C. in an architect's open plan office

    D. during naptime at a nursery school

26. Calculate the number of heating degree days during the following two-week period in March in Williamsburg, Virginia. The base temperature is 65°F (18°C).

date	high	low	average
3/1	51°F (11°C)	31°F (−1°C)	41°F (5°C)
3/2	79°F (26°C)	39°F (4°C)	59°F (15°C)
3/3	51°F (11°C)	35°F (2°C)	43°F (6°C)
3/4	53°F (12°C)	31°F (−1°C)	42°F (5°C)
3/5	54°F (12°C)	34°F (1°C)	44°F (6°C)
3/6	46°F (8°C)	36°F (2°C)	41°F (5°C)
3/7	51°F (11°C)	27°F (−3°C)	39°F (4°C)
3/8	58°F (14°C)	23°F (−5°C)	40°F (4°C)
3/9	72°F (22°C)	49°F (9°C)	60°F (15°C)
3/10	78°F (26°C)	63°F (17°C)	70°F (21°C)
3/11	70°F (21°C)	52°F (11°C)	61°F (16°C)
3/12	69°F (21°C)	55°F (13°C)	62°F (17°C)
3/13	75°F (24°C)	55°F (13°C)	65°F (18°C)
3/14	70°F (21°C)	54°F (12°C)	62°F (16°C)

    A. 179 heating degree days F (99 heating degree days C)

    B. 186 heating degree days F (102 heating degree days C)

    C. 230 heating degree days F (128 heating degree days C)

    D. 316 heating degree days F (176 heating degree days C)

27. Which type of HVAC system would be the best choice for a large building where a need for simultaneous heating and cooling is expected?

    A. direct expansion

    B. variable air volume

    C. dual duct

    D. reheat system

28. The energy cost budget method, as defined in ASHRAE/IESNA 90.1, would be recommended for all of the following types of buildings EXCEPT

    A. a building that utilizes passive solar heating

    B. a convenience store operating 24 hours a day, seven days a week

    C. an office building powered with photovoltaic panels

    D. a building with no mechanical system

29. A company is considering replacing its existing HVAC system with a new system at a total cost of $55,000. It is expected that the new, more efficient system will save the company $460 per month in utility costs. The simple payback period of their investment would be _____ years. (Fill in the blank.)

30. An architect is researching folding partitions to be specified to divide a hotel ballroom into two smaller meeting rooms. Meetings will frequently be held in each of the rooms simultaneously, and the presenters often use a lavaliere microphone with an amplification system. The hotel's facilities coordinator specifies that normal speech should not be heard from the other side of the partition, but it is acceptable for loud or amplified speech to be faintly heard. Into which range should the partition's STC rating fall?

    A. 25 to 30

    B. 30 to 35

    C. 35 to 40

    D. 40 to 45

31. Determine the total absorption of an office 12 ft (4 m) wide and 15 ft (5 m) long with a 9 ft (3 m) ceiling. Each window is 5 ft (1.5 m) tall and 3 ft (1 m) wide. Assume that the door is sealed and the door assembly has the same noise reduction coefficient (NRC) as the wall assembly.

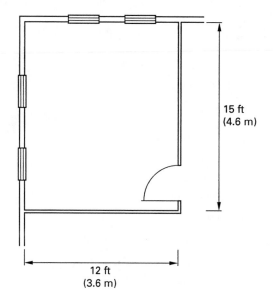

15 ft (4.6 m)

12 ft (3.6 m)

surface	description	NRC
walls	½ in (13) gypsum board on metal studs at 16 in (406) o.c.	0.05
ceiling	acoustical ceiling tile	0.60
floor	carpet on pad	0.55
windows	standard window glass	0.15

    A. 225.3 sabins (ft²) (25.0 sabins (m²))

    B. 237.3 sabins (ft²) (26.3 sabins (m²))

    C. 240.3 sabins (ft²) (26.6 sabins (m²))

    D. 245.3 sabins (ft²) (27.2 sabins (m²))

32. What is the minimum desirable width (x) of the lobby shown?

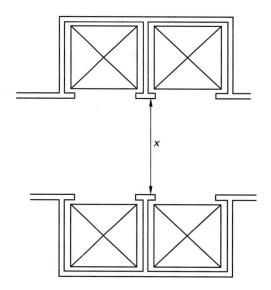

x

A.   8 ft (2.5 m)

B.   10 ft (3.0 m)

C.   12 ft (3.7 m)

D.   14 ft (4.3 m)

33.   Which of the following devices is used to depressurize a space to test for air infiltration?

A.   a nanometer

B.   a blower door

C.   a flow hood

D.   a duct blower

34.   Which of the following types of conduit is best suited for use when connecting to a motor?

A.   flexible metal conduit

B.   electric metallic tubing

C.   intermediate metal conduit

D.   rigid steel conduit

35.   What is the voltage of the service obtained at each tap?

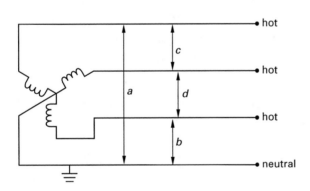

A. $a = 120$ V, $b = 120$ V, $c = 240$ V, and $d = 240$ V

B. $a = 277$ V, $b = 277$ V, $c = 480$ V, and $d = 480$ V

C. $a = 208$ V, $b = 208$ V, $c = 120$ V, and $d = 120$ V

D. $a = 120$ V, $b = 120$ V, $c = 208$ V, and $d = 208$ V

36.   An architect is designing a nursing home with 150 beds. The patients have varying levels of mobility and independence. The building manager requests an HVAC system that permits each patient to control the temperature in his or her own room, that is quiet, and that requires minimal maintenance. Which type of system would be the most appropriate recommendation?

A.   packaged terminal units

B.   fan coil terminals

C.   variable air volume

D.   single duct, constant air volume

37.   Which of the following principles is best exemplified by the "whispering arch" at Union Station in St. Louis, Missouri?

A.   focusing

B.   creep

C.   diffusion

D.   specular reflection

38.   Identify the following electrical symbols.

I.   a. exit sign

II.   b. home run to panel board

III.   c. computer data outlet

IV.   d. duplex floor receptacle

A.   I = c, II = d, III = b, and IV = a

B.   I = d, II = c, III = a, and IV = b

C.   I = c, II = d, III = a, and IV = b

D.   I = a, II = d, III = b, and IV = c

39.   Mrs. Jones plans to wash and dry a load of white laundry, a load of colors, a load of towels, and a load of sheets. Her washing machine uses 750 W of electricity, and each wash cycle lasts 45 min. Her dryer uses 5000 W of electricity, and it will take 1 hr to dry each load of laundry. When the clothes are clean and dry, Mrs. Jones will spend an hour ironing. Her iron uses 800 W of electricity.

The Jones family pays $0.08/kW-hr for electricity. How much will the electricity cost that's needed to wash, dry, and iron the laundry?

   A. $1.56
   B. $1.84
   C. $2.12
   D. $2.30

40.   Which of the following statements regarding conduit embedded in concrete slabs is FALSE?

   A.   The minimum concrete cover over conduit should be at least $3/4$ in (19).
   B.   Conduit should always be placed in the lower half of the structural slab.
   C.   The outside diameter of the conduit should be no larger than $1/3$ of the thickness of the slab.
   D.   Aluminum conduit may be used instead of steel conduit when it is fully embedded within a concrete slab.

41.   Which of the following spaces should be acoustically "live"? (Choose the two that apply.)

   A.   a talk radio recording studio
   B.   a cathedral featuring an antique German pipe organ
   C.   an opera house
   D.   a community playhouse often used for poetry recitation
   E.   a university lecture hall
   F.   a movie theater

42.   The section of the soil stack that is located above the highest plumbing fixture in a building is called the

   A.   vent stack
   B.   stack vent
   C.   cleanout
   D.   vacuum breaker

43.   In case of a fire, which of these can be activated by building occupants? (Choose the three that apply.)

   A.   fire extinguishers
   B.   dry standpipes
   C.   wet standpipes
   D.   fusible links
   E.   annunciators
   F.   two-way communications devices

44.   A sound composed of only one frequency is known as a

   A.   chord
   B.   tone
   C.   note
   D.   pitch

45.   Which type of fire extinguisher should be provided in an electrical room?

   A.   class A
   B.   class B
   C.   class C
   D.   class D

46.   Which of the following formulas is NOT a factor in determining cooling load?

   A. $q_r = (SG)(SC)A$
   B. $q_m = 1500(BHP)$
   C. $q_{CLTD} = UA(CLTD)$
   D. $q_c = UA\Delta T$

47.   Electric baseboard heaters transfer heat through

   A.   radiation
   B.   convection
   C.   conduction
   D.   evaporation

48.   Identify the following incandescent lamp shapes.

I.

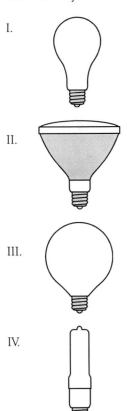

II.

III.

IV.

    A.   I–A, II–R, III–P, IV–T
    B.   I–A, II–PAR, III–G, IV–T
    C.   I–T, II–R, III–P, IV–B
    D.   I–T, II–PAR, III–G, IV–A

49.   On a busy New York City street with a decibel level of 90, a cab driver blows his horn. The decibel level of the horn is 95. What is the total sound intensity level?

    A.   91 dB
    B.   91.2 dB
    C.   96.2 dB
    D.   185 dB

50.   Which are the areas of negative wind pressure in and around the building in the following illustration? (Choose the three that apply.)

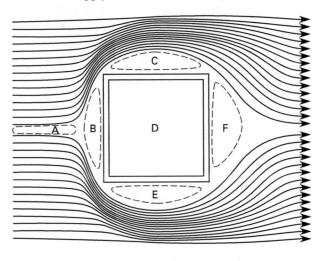

Used with permission from Fuller Moore, Environmental Control Systems: Heating Cooling Lighting, copyright © 2004, by Fuller Moore.

51.   Which natural cooling technique is utilized by the Pantheon?

    A.   stack ventilation
    B.   pools of water
    C.   thermal mass
    D.   cross ventilation

52.   Which of the following does NOT have a significant effect on a person's level of thermal comfort?

    A.   age
    B.   activity level
    C.   clothing
    D.   relative humidity

53. What is the most likely location for a vernacular American home with the following first-floor plan?

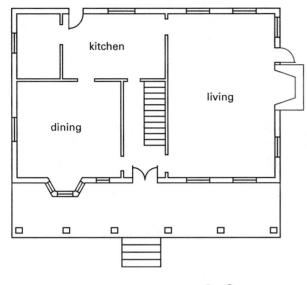

kitchen

living

dining

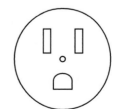

A. Vermont
B. Louisiana
C. Montana
D. Maryland

54. Which material has the greatest specific heat?

A. concrete
B. water
C. adobe
D. gypsum

55. In the event of an emergency, which of the following elevator safety mechanisms will activate first?

A. spring buffers
B. safety rail clamps
C. centrifugal governor
D. final-limit switches

56. Production of which of the following refrigerants has been banned in the United States? (Choose the two that apply.)

A. Halon
B. CFC
C. HFC
D. HCFC
E. VOC
F. Freon

57. The uppermost curved line on the psychrometric chart represents

A. humidity ratio
B. enthalpy
C. saturated air
D. specific volume

58. Identify the range receptacle.

A.

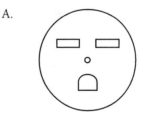

B.

C.

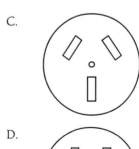

D.

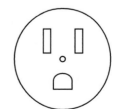

59.   What is an escalator's typical travel speed?

    A.   50 ft/min (15 m/min)

    B.   75 ft/min (23 m/min)

    C.   100 ft/min (30 m/min)

    D.   150 ft/min (48 m/min)

60.   Which of the following statements regarding escalators is true?

    A.   An escalator can be counted as a means of egress.

    B.   Structural support is required at both ends and at intermediate bracing points.

    C.   Emergency power is required for all escalators.

    D.   All escalators are installed at an angle of 30° from horizontal.

61.   A school is planned for a site near a major interstate. In addition to sound attenuation strategies to be incorporated into the building design, what site planting strategy would most reduce the amount of highway noise reaching the school?

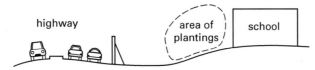

    A.   planting deciduous trees and low shrubs

    B.   planting evergreen trees

    C.   planting deciduous trees

    D.   planting a combination of deciduous and evergreen trees

62.   An architect is working on a preliminary planning study for an elementary school. The school is being designed for 750 students: 400 girls and 350 boys. From the sample code below, a total of _____ water closets are required. (Fill in the blank.)

> **Plumbing fixture requirements for pupils' use:**
> water closets:
>   1 per 100 males
>   1 per 35 females
> lavatories:
>   1 per 50 students
> urinals:
>   1 per 30 male students
> drinking fountains:
>   1 per 150 students

63.   To minimize glare, the brightness ratio between a task and its adjacent surroundings should be limited to approximately

    A. $1:\frac{1}{2}$

    B. $1:\frac{1}{3}$

    C. $1:\frac{1}{5}$

    D. $1:\frac{1}{10}$

64.   Values in the area indicated on the following psychrometric chart call for

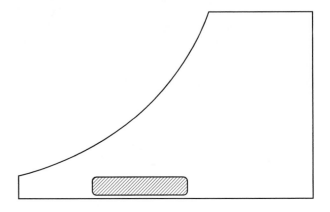

    A.   dehumidification

    B.   evaporative cooling

    C.   passive solar heating

    D.   humidification

65.   Assuming that the capacity of each type of plant is the same, which type of HVAC system occupies the most space within the building?

    A.   forced air

    B.   radiant

    C.   hydronic

    D.   unitary

66.   Which of the following is NOT a factor in zonal cavity method calculations?

    A.   area of the space

    B.   ceiling height

    C.   maintenance schedules for fixtures

    D.   coefficient of utilization

67. A three-phase motor draws a 9 A current at 208 V. The power factor is 75%. The power generated is

    A. 1.4 kW
    B. 2.4 kW
    C. 3.6 kW
    D. 4.2 kW

68. A doctor is building a new clinic in a rural area. The building will be dependent upon a private water source, and the well is approximately 150 ft (45.7 m) deep. What type of well pump would be an appropriate choice?

    A. suction pump
    B. turbine pump
    C. submersible pump
    D. venturi pump

69. Which of the following is NOT a characteristic of vertical displacement ventilation design?

    A. stratified room air
    B. quiet distribution system
    C. drafts
    D. reduced cooling capacity necessary

70. Which of the following buildings would be a good application of demand-controlled ventilation technology?

    A. a pet store
    B. a locker room
    C. a bowling alley
    D. a dry cleaner

71. Which of the following is a type of perimeter security system?

    A. photoelectric cells
    B. pressure sensors
    C. ultrasonic detectors
    D. photoelectric beams

72. The minimum SEER rating required for all new residential air conditioning units manufactured in the United States is _____. (Fill in the blank.)

73. Which of the following is LEAST likely to be included in a typical transformer specification?

    A. sound level in decibels
    B. the type of cooling medium
    C. physical dimensions
    D. voltage

74. Which of the following receptacle locations would NOT require GFCI protection?

    A. an exterior receptacle for holiday lights
    B. a coffeemaker receptacle on a kitchen counter
    C. a receptacle located in a finished living area in a basement
    D. a receptacle for a chest freezer located in a garage

75. Installing a sprinkler system in new construction increases the total construction cost by approximately

    A. 1.5%
    B. 5%
    C. 9%
    D. 15%

76. Which of the following statements is FALSE?

    A. 14-gage wire is the smallest gage that should be used for building wiring.
    B. Circuits for motors should be oversized by 25%.
    C. The rotational speed of a three-phase induction motor remains constant.
    D. All fixtures and receptacles in a room should be on the same circuit.

77. Which elevator operating system would be the most appropriate choice for a four-story luxury apartment building with two passenger elevators?

    A. selective collective operation
    B. computerized system control
    C. single automatic push-button control
    D. collective control

78. Determine an appropriate spacing for ceiling diffusers in the space shown.

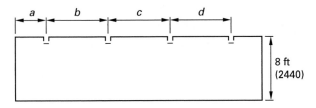

not to scale

A. $a = 3$ ft (910), $b = 6$ ft (1830), $c = 6$ ft (1830), $d = 6$ ft (1830)

B. $a = 2$ ft (610), $b = 4$ ft (1220), $c = 4$ ft (1220), $d = 4$ ft (1220)

C. $a = 4$ ft (1220), $b = 8$ ft (2440), $c = 8$ ft (2440), $d = 8$ ft (2440)

D. $a = 3$ ft (910), $b = 6$ ft (1830), $c = 8$ ft (2440), $d = 6$ ft (1830)

79. Which of the following is NOT required of lavatories to meet ADAAG guidelines?

A. The rim shall be no more than 34 in (865) above the finish floor.

B. Clear floor space of 30 in (760) by 48 in (1220) must be provided in front of the lavatory.

C. All piping must be concealed within cabinetry.

D. The bowl of the sink must be no greater than $6^1/_2$ in (165) deep.

80. A curtain board is

A. used to block sunlight entering a space

B. a part of a suspended wall assembly

C. used to restrict movement of smoke and flame

D. used to direct light toward the ceiling for even, reflected illumination

81. Which type of fixture is assigned the greatest number of fixture units?

A. a lavatory

B. a flush-valve water closet

C. a washing machine

D. a flush-tank water closet

82. Which type of photovoltaic cell produces the most power?

A. thin-film

B. crystalline

C. polycrystalline

D. amorphous

83. Which approaches would be appropriate for passively cooling a building in Taos, New Mexico?

I. evaporative cooler

II. roof ponds

III. using building materials with high thermal mass

IV. courtyards with fountains

A. I and II only

B. I and III only

C. II, III, and IV only

D. I, II, III, and IV

84. Which of the following statements is FALSE?

A. The absorption coefficient of a room should be between 0.20 and 0.50.

B. To produce a clearly noticeable reduction in noise, the absorption in a room should be doubled.

C. Even a small hole in a 10 ft by 10 ft (3 m by 3 m) partition, such as that caused by unsealed electrical receptacles placed back to back, can make the partition effectively useless for blocking sound.

D. In large rooms, absorptive treatments applied to the ceiling are more effective than wall treatments.

85. An architect is planning a 100,000 ft² (10 000 m²) university classroom building. The mechanical engineer estimates that the total floor area required for the boiler room and the chilled water plant will be about 3000 ft² (300 m²). Which of the following criteria should also be kept in mind when determining the location and design of the mechanical rooms? (Choose the three that apply.)

A. Each mechanical room should have at least one exterior wall.

B. The boiler room should be adjacent to the chilled water plant.

C. Rooms should be as square as possible.

D. Ceilings in both rooms should be at least 12 ft (3.7 m) high.

E. Mechanical rooms must be placed on the ground floor.

F. The mechanical rooms should be equal in size.

86. Plumbing fixtures in large buildings are often placed back to back, and restrooms are stacked from floor to floor. In the typical restroom layout shown, how much clear space (x) should be allowed within the plumbing wall? All fixtures are wall hung.

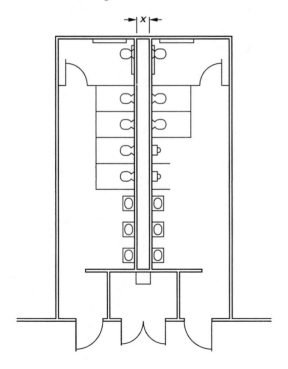

A. 12 in (305)
B. 16 in (406)
C. 18 in (457)
D. 24 in (610)

87. Which of the following are expected results of a properly designed and implemented building commissioning plan? (Choose the four that apply.)

A. increased energy efficiency

B. a comprehensive training program for maintenance staff

C. verification of 100% of the building systems by the commissioning agent

D. operation and maintenance manuals delivered to the owner in a useful and organized format

E. record drawings for all HVAC and electrical components

F. improved indoor air quality

88. Which chart most accurately represents the distribution of energy use for a large office building?

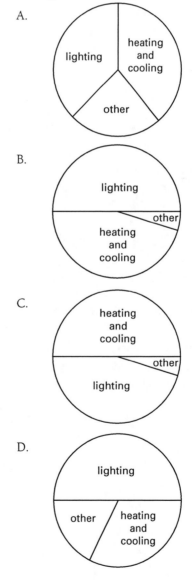

89. Which of the following statements about fiber optics is FALSE?

    A. Fiber optics is predominantly used in the telecommunications industry.

    B. There is a greater signal loss with fiber than with copper cables.

    C. Single-mode fiber optics has more capacity for transmitting information than multimode fiber.

    D. Fiber optics uses light pulses to transmit information.

90. Which of the following is NOT an effective remedy for sick building syndrome?

    A. Increase the quantity of outdoor air in the HVAC system.

    B. Provide task ventilation in areas with high concentrations of odor or chemicals.

    C. Thoroughly clean the entire HVAC system.

    D. Incorporate live plants into the interior design of the building.

91. Which of the following building types would have the highest percentage of total construction cost allocated for HVAC?

    A. a full-service, sit-down restaurant

    B. a climate controlled mini-warehouse

    C. a hospital

    D. a parking garage

92. Which of the following statements regarding transformers is FALSE?

    A. Transformers cannot be used with direct current.

    B. Substation transformers can be pole-mounted.

    C. Higher grades of insulation in combination with an underrated transformer can decrease lifetime operating costs.

    D. Transformers installed indoors are usually dry type.

93. An array of photovoltaic panels in the northern hemisphere should be mounted facing

    A. north

    B. south

    C. east

    D. west

94. Which of the following is NOT a recommended connection for a three-phase transformer?

    A. delta to delta

    B. delta to wye

    C. wye to delta

    D. wye to wye

95. A high school teacher is standing at the front of a classroom delivering a lecture to a class of 25 students. Students in the front row, 3 ft (1 m) in front of the teacher's lectern, perceive the teacher's voice at 65 dB. What is the decibel level of the teacher's voice in the back row, 12 ft (4 m) from the lectern?

    A. 53 dB

    B. 56 dB

    C. 59 dB

    D. 65 dB

PRACTICE EXAM: VIGNETTE

MECHANICAL AND ELECTRICAL PLAN

Directions

Complete the provided reflected ceiling plan for a small travel agency using the symbols given. The solution must show a ceiling grid for acoustical tile, lighting fixtures, and a schematic representation of the HVAC plan, including air diffusers, return air grilles, ductwork, and fire dampers. Locate light fixtures to achieve the required light level indicated in the program using the light distribution diagrams provided. The lighting layout should minimize overlighting and underlighting and provide for maximum flexibility for furniture layouts.

Program

Suspended Ceiling System

1. Provide a 2 ft by 4 ft (600 by 1200) grid with lay-in acoustical tiles in all spaces.
2. The ceiling height in all spaces is 9 ft 0 in (2740).
3. Interior partitions terminate 4 in (100) above the finished ceiling. Fire-rated partitions and bearing walls extend to the bottom of the floor deck above.

Lighting System

1. Lighting layouts should provide for efficient, uniform illumination. For all spaces except the reception area, use only recessed fluorescent fixtures to provide uniform light distribution with a light level of approximately 50 fc (500 lx) measured at approximately 2 ft 6 in (760) above the floor.
2. For the reception area, use only recessed compact fluorescent downlights to provide uniform light distribution with a light level of approximately 50 fc (500 lx) measured at approximately 2 ft 6 in (760) above the floor.
3. In addition to the general lighting required above, provide accent light fixtures along the north wall of the executive office. To achieve the desired effect, the direct light level should be 70 fc (700 lx) at 5 ft 0 in (1500) above the floor. The fixture specification states that this illumination can be achieved by spacing fixtures 4 ft 0 in (1200) on center and locating them 2 ft 0 in (600) from the wall.
4. Provide exit signs at all egress doors.

HVAC System

The space is served by supply air and return air risers in the shaft shown on the plan. Supply air is provided through ductwork. Return air grilles are open to the plenum. However, the plenum must be connected to the return air riser with rigid ductwork. The HVAC system should provide for uniform air distribution with an economical duct layout conforming to the following.

1. Provide a minimum of one supply air diffuser and one return air grille in each space. An acceptable distribution pattern includes one supply air diffuser and one return air grille for every 150 ft² (14 m²) of floor area or fraction thereof.
2. Each supply air diffuser must be connected to the rigid supply duct system with flexible ducts. Flexible ducts may not exceed 10 ft (3050) in length. Each diffuser must have a separate flexible duct connecting it to the rigid duct system.
3. Flexible ducts may fit through joist webs.
4. Rigid ducts fit under beams, in spaces between joists, and in a zone that extends 2 ft (600) from the beams and bearing walls in plan view. Rigid ducts do not fit through joist webs or between the bottoms of joists and the ceiling except within the 2 ft (600) zone mentioned previously.
5. Duct openings in fire-rated partitions must be protected with fire dampers.

Tips

- Be familiar with the contents of each layer.
- On the actual exam, use the *move, adjust* tool and click anywhere within the grid to shift the cells within the perimeter of the grid rectangle.
- On the actual exam, use the *move, adjust* tool and click on the edge of the grid rectangle to increase or decrease the length or width of the entire grid rectangle.
- On the actual exam, use the *move group* tool and click on any part of the grid to move the entire grid rectangle elsewhere.
- If one element of two overlapping elements cannot be selected, keep clicking without moving the mouse until the desired element is highlighted.

Tools

Useful tools include the following.

- *zoom* tool for laying out the ceiling grid
- *rotate* tool for rotating the ceiling grid
- *sketch measure* tool to check for spacing distances from walls

Target Time: 1 hour

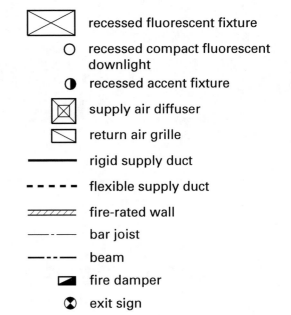

MECHANICAL AND ELECTRICAL SYMBOLS

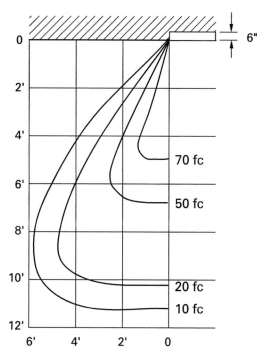

footcandle distribution for recessed
fluorescent fixtures–U.S. units

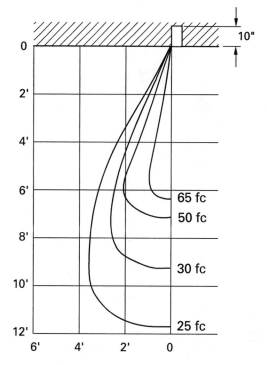

footcandle distribution for recessed compact
fluorescent downlights–U.S. units

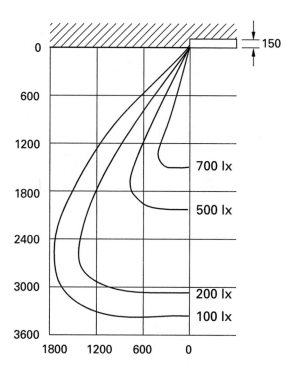

footcandle distribution for recessed
fluorescent fixtures–SI units

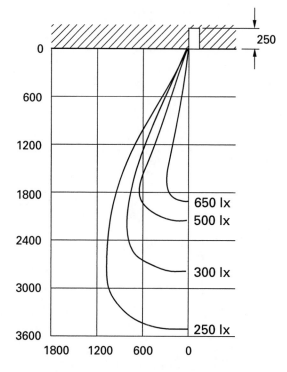

footcandle distribution for recessed compact
fluorescent downlights–SI units

LIGHT DISTRIBUTION DIAGRAMS

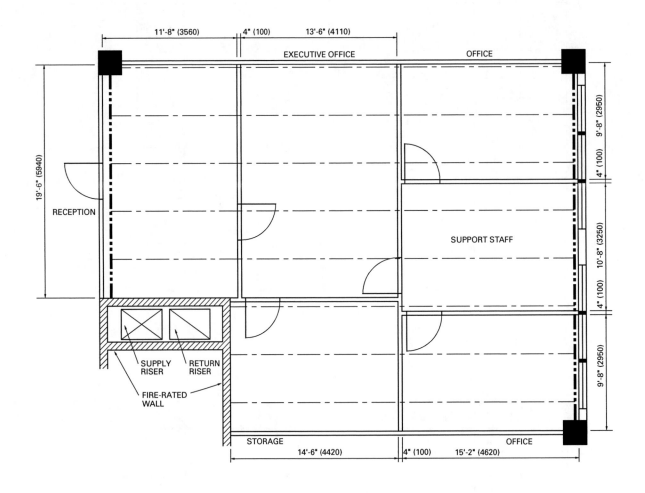

RECEPTION

EXECUTIVE OFFICE

OFFICE

SUPPORT STAFF

SUPPLY RISER

RETURN RISER

FIRE-RATED WALL

STORAGE

OFFICE

11'-8" (3560)   4" (100)   13'-6" (4110)

19'-6" (5940)

9'-8" (2950)   4" (100)   10'-8" (3250)   4" (100)   9'-8" (2950)

14'-6" (4420)   4" (100)   15'-2" (4620)

Scale: 1/8" = 1'-0"
[1:100 metric]

MECHANICAL AND ELECTRICAL PLAN

PRACTICE EXAM: MULTIPLE CHOICE SOLUTIONS

1. (A) ● (C) (D)
2. (A) (B) ● (D)
3. (A) (B) ● (D)
4. ● (B) (C) (D)
5. _____ **3 tons** _____
6. (A) (B) (C) ●
7. (A) (B) (C) ●
8. ● (B) (C) (D)
9. (A) (B) ● (D)
10. (A) ● (C) (D)
11. ● (B) (C) (D)
12. (A) (B) (C) ●
13. (A) (B) ● (D)
14. _____ **79 cd/ft² (79 cd/m²)** _____
15. (A) (B) (C) ●
16. (A) (B) ● (D)
17. (A) ● (C) (D)
18. ●(B)(C)(D)●(F)
19. (A) (B) (C) ●
20. ● (B) (C) (D)
21. (A) ● (C) (D)
22. (A) (B) ● (D)
23. (A) (B) (C) ●
24. (A) ● (C) (D)
25. (A) ● (C) (D)

26. (A) ● (C) (D)
27. (A) (B) ● (D)
28. (A) (B) (C) ●
29. _____ **10 years** _____
30. (A) (B) (C) ●
31. (A) ● (C) (D)
32. (A) ● (C) (D)
33. (A) ● (C) (D)
34. ● (B) (C) (D)
35. (A) (B) (C) ●
36. (A) (B) ● (D)
37. ● (B) (C) (D)
38. ● (B) (C) (D)
39. (A) ● (C) (D)
40. (A) (B) (C) ●
41. (A)●●(D)(E)(F)
42. (A) ● (C) (D)
43. ●(B)●(D)(E)●
44. (A) ● (C) (D)
45. (A) (B) ● (D)
46. (A) (B) (C) ●
47. (A) ● (C) (D)
48. (A) ● (C) (D)
49. (A) (B) ● (D)
50. (A)(B)●(D)●●

51. ● (B) (C) (D)
52. ● (B) (C) (D)
53. (A) (B) (C) ●
54. (A) ● (C) (D)
55. (A) (B) ● (D)
56. ●●(C)(D)(E)(F)
57. (A) (B) ● (D)
58. (A) (B) ● (D)
59. (A) (B) ● (D)
60. (A) (B) (C) ●
61. (A) (B) (C) ●
62. _____ **16 water closets** _____
63. (A) ● (C) (D)
64. (A) (B) (C) ●
65. ● (B) (C) (D)
66. (A) ● (C) (D)
67. (A) ● (C) (D)
68. (A) (B) ● (D)
69. (A) (B) ● (D)
70. (A) (B) ● (D)
71. ● (B) (C) (D)
72. _____ **13** _____
73. (A) (B) ● (D)
74. (A) (B) ● (D)
75. ● (B) (C) (D)

76. Ⓐ Ⓑ Ⓒ ⬤   86. Ⓐ Ⓑ Ⓒ ⬤
77. ⬤ Ⓑ Ⓒ Ⓓ   87. ⬤⬤Ⓒ⬤Ⓔ⬤
78. Ⓐ Ⓑ ⬤ Ⓓ   88. Ⓐ Ⓑ Ⓒ ⬤
79. Ⓐ Ⓑ ⬤ Ⓓ   89. Ⓐ ⬤ Ⓒ Ⓓ
80. Ⓐ Ⓑ ⬤ Ⓓ   90. Ⓐ Ⓑ Ⓒ ⬤
81. Ⓐ ⬤ Ⓒ Ⓓ   91. ⬤ Ⓑ Ⓒ Ⓓ
82. Ⓐ ⬤ Ⓒ Ⓓ   92. Ⓐ ⬤ Ⓒ Ⓓ
83. Ⓐ Ⓑ ⬤ Ⓓ   93. Ⓐ ⬤ Ⓒ Ⓓ
84. Ⓐ ⬤ Ⓒ Ⓓ   94. Ⓐ Ⓑ Ⓒ ⬤
85. ⬤⬤Ⓒ⬤ⒺⒻ   95. ⬤ Ⓑ Ⓒ Ⓓ

1. The answer is B.

Duct sizes are determined by calculating the cross-sectional area required to accommodate a certain amount of air at a given velocity and then choosing a shape that provides that cross-sectional area and will fit within the space allotted for mechanical pathways through the building. The formula for calculating cross-sectional area is

In U.S. units:

$$A_{in^2} = \left(\frac{\text{volume of air in cfm}}{\text{velocity in fpm}}\right) (\text{friction allowance})$$

$$\times \left(144 \frac{in^2}{ft^2}\right)$$

In SI units:

$$A_{m^2} = \left(\frac{\text{volume of air in m}^3/\text{s}}{\text{velocity in m/s}}\right) (\text{friction allowance})$$

In this problem, the most important variable is *friction allowance*. Friction allowances vary depending on the shape of the duct; larger, roomier ducts have lower friction allowances than more constricted shapes. A round shape has the least surface area for the same cross-sectional area. Ducts with smooth rounded shapes offer less resistance than ducts with tight spaces or sharp corners. A round duct has a friction allowance of 1.0, making it the least resistive choice; therefore, it is the most desirable.

If round ducts are not feasible, the next best choice is a square or nearly square cross section. Small square ducts (less than 1000 cfm [0.5 m³/s]) have a friction allowance of 1.10, while larger ones have a friction allowance of 1.05. Thin rectangular ducts are the most restrictive and have a friction allowance of 1.25.

2. The answer is C.

Embodied energy is a measurement of the amount of energy consumed to produce a specific amount of a material. Plywood has the lowest amount of embodied energy relative to the other materials on the list. One square foot of ³⁄₈ in (9.53) plywood requires about 5500 Btu (5800 kJ) for production.

Plywood is made by harvesting trees, peeling the flitches from the logs, and laminating them into a sheet. Energy is used to power the saws; to fuel the trucks that take the logs from the forest to the sawmill; to operate the machines that slice the logs, stack the plies, and glue them together; and to deliver the finished product to the job site.

Compare that to the process of making tempered glass, which requires about 72,600 Btu/ft² (824 000 kJ/m²). The sand is first extracted from a quarry. The components must then be combined and heated until molten, floated on molten tin, solidified, and then heated again in the tempering process. A tremendous amount of energy is required for each of these heat-driven processes, so tempered glass has much more embodied energy than plywood.

The values are even higher for metals, such as steel and aluminum, and for materials like ceramic tile, which is fired to make it hard and resilient.

3. The answer is C.

The *hypothalamus* acts as a thermostat within the human body. It regulates the distribution of blood to react to changes in external temperature sensed by the nerves in the skin and to changes in internal body temperature caused by exertion or illness. The hypothalamus either dilates or constricts blood vessels to allow more or less blood, respectively, to flow toward the surface of the body. It also controls other reactions to temperature, such as goose bumps and shivering.

4. The answer is A.

The *U*-value, or thermal transmittance, is equivalent to the reciprocal of the sum of the *R*-values (RSI-values) of the materials and airspaces that make up the assembly. To solve this problem, list the materials and determine the *R*-values (RSI-values) for the thicknesses given. Note that some of the *R*-values (RSI-values) are given for the total thickness of the materials, and others are given as *R*-value per inch (RSI-value per meter). It's easiest to ensure that they are all included by listing them in order from interior to exterior or vice versa. In this case, the stud is excluded because the *R*-value (RSI-value) is calculated at a point between the studs as indicated on the plan. (Don't forget the interior and exterior air layers.)

material	R-value (ft²-hr-°F/Btu)	RSI-value (m²·°C/W)
inside air layer	0.68	0.12
⁵⁄₈ in (16) gypsum wallboard	0.56	0.10
plastic film vapor barrier	–	–
3¹⁄₂ in (89) batt insulation (3.5 × 3.3 [0.089 × 23])	11.55	2.05
1¹⁄₂ in (38) airspace	0.61	0.11
3⁵⁄₈ in (92) brick (3.625 × 0.30 [0.092 × 2.1])	1.09	0.19
outside air layer	0.17	0.03

In U.S. units:

The sum of the *R*-values is 14.66 ft²-hr-°F/Btu. The *U*-value is the reciprocal of that, or

$$U = \frac{1}{R} = \frac{1}{14.66 \dfrac{\text{ft}^2 \text{-hr-°F}}{\text{Btu}}} = 0.068 \text{ Btu/ft}^2\text{-hr-°F}$$

In SI units:

The sum of the RSI-values is 2.6 m²·°C/W. The *U*-value is the reciprocal of that, or

$$U = \frac{1}{\text{RSI}} = \frac{1}{2.6 \dfrac{\text{m}^2 \cdot \text{°C}}{\text{W}}} = 0.38 \text{ W/m}^2 \cdot \text{°C}$$

5.   The answer is 3 tons.

A good guideline when selecting a cooling system for an older home is to assume that approximately 1 ton of cooling capacity will be necessary for each 500 ft² (46 m²) of living space. This old farmhouse presumably has drafty windows and lots of air infiltration, so a 3 ton unit would be a reasonable choice.

If this project were a residence of similar size but new construction, a more appropriate guideline would be about 1 ton for each 1000 ft² (93 m²) of floor area. New construction materials and methods, such as house wrap and vapor barriers, additional insulation, improved windows, caulking and sealants, and so on, make it much easier to control the environment within the residence and require less cooling capacity.

6.   The answer is D.

The strategy pictured is *direct gain*. Heat from the sun passing through the window is absorbed by the mass of the concrete and distributed throughout the space.

7.   The answer is D.

A *zeolite process* is not used to disinfect potable water. It is used to soften water that has a high mineral content.

Chlorination is the most common process used to disinfect drinking water. The chlorine kills bacteria and viruses that may be in the water. *Ozonation* and exposure to *ultraviolet light* are two other methods of removing harmful organisms from drinking water.

8.   The answer is A.

A *lightning protection system* is designed to provide a continuous path from a building (most often from the highest points of the building) to the ground. Unfortunately, no method exists for preventing lightning strikes. The best that can be achieved is to route the energy from the strike to a point where the strike is least likely to damage mechanical, electrical, and computer systems or cause a fire.

9.   The answer is C.

A *preaction* sprinkler system would be a good choice for the store. Preaction systems admit water to the sprinkler pipes after the system detects a fire. As the water enters the pipes, the system sounds an alarm. The delay between detection and activation allows a little time for the fire to be found and extinguished before the sprinkler heads open. This type of system is a popular choice for applications where there would be a great deal of water damage to building contents if the sprinklers were activated.

Wet pipe systems are always filled with water and are activated by the sprinkler heads through use of a fusible link or other heat sensitive controls. The water is immediately discharged in the area where the fire is detected. *Dry pipe* systems are filled with compressed air until the system is activated, and then water fills the pipes and exits through the sprinkler heads. They are a good choice for unheated buildings where water in the pipes could potentially freeze and render the system useless. A *deluge* system is filled with water, like a wet pipe system, but all of the heads discharge at the same time. They are used where flammable materials are stored, or where a fire could spread very rapidly. However, if the system activates, the potential for severe water damage is high.

10.   The answer is B.

Photoelectric smoke detectors (like the ones often found in homes) pass a beam of light onto a sensor; if the beam is obscured by smoke, the alarm sounds. Smoke begins to form when a fire reaches the smoldering stage.

11.   The answer is A.

When a portion of a building is under construction or undergoing renovation, smoke detector covers should be used to protect the detectors from damage, from accumulating dust that could destroy the sensors, and from sounding false alarms.

Ionization detectors would be a poor choice for a restaurant kitchen or any other location that tends to be hot, because of the high likelihood of false alarms.

Smoke detectors are normally installed in ductwork to direct the HVAC system to shut down in case of a fire, so that smoke and other toxic gases are not transported throughout the building through the ventilation system. They are not an acceptable substitute for detector systems installed throughout the occupied areas of the building.

Of all types of detectors, spot heat detectors would detect a fire last, and after the most deadly smoke stage. They detect changes in the temperature of the space.

12.   **The answer is D.**

The *declination angle* is the angle of the earth's axis in comparison to the position of the sun.

Altitude and *azimuth angles* describe the location of the sun in relationship to a specific point on the earth. Altitude is the height of the sun above the ground. Azimuth is the sun's compass orientation.

Profile angle is the angle of the shadow that is cast by an overhang.

13.   **The answer is C.**

The Energy Policy Act of 1992 requires all new showerheads in the United States to dispense a maximum of 2.5 gal (9.5 L) of water per minute.

The act requires that all new toilets use a maximum of 1.6 gal (6.1 L) of water per flush and that urinals use a maximum of 1.0 gal (3.8 L) per flush. It also specifies maximum consumption rates for faucets and aerators, which may dispense 2.5 gal (9.5 L) of water per minute.

Fixtures that use less than the maximums are permitted and encouraged. New technologies have made it possible to reduce potable water consumption even further than the act's requirements. Waterless urinals and dual flush toilets reduce the quantities of water needed for eliminating waste. Some municipalities permit the use of *graywater* (wastewater from other fixtures that contains no organic matter) or captured rainwater for flushing toilets. Composting toilets are also available that use no water at all. Specifying sensors on faucets and toilets can also reduce the amount of potable water consumed.

14.   **The answer is 79 cd/ft² (79 cd/m²).**

In U.S. units:

The *illuminance* of the wall is calculated from the luminous intensity, I, and the distance between the light source and the wall.

$$E = \frac{I}{d^2} = \frac{2500 \text{ cd}}{(5 \text{ ft})^2} = 100 \text{ cd/ft}^2$$

The *luminance* of the wall is equal to the illuminance multiplied by the reflectance factor, R.

$$L = ER = \left(100 \frac{\text{cd}}{\text{ft}^2}\right)(0.79) = 79 \text{ cd/ft}^2$$

In SI units:

The *illuminance* of the wall is calculated from the luminous intensity, I, and the distance between the light source and the wall.

$$E = \frac{I}{d^2} = \frac{2500 \text{ cd}}{(5 \text{ m})^2} = 100 \text{ cd/m}^2$$

The *luminance* of the wall is equal to the illuminance multiplied by the reflectance factor, R.

$$L = ER = \left(100 \frac{\text{cd}}{\text{m}^2}\right)(0.79) = 79 \text{ cd/m}^2$$

15.   **The answer is D.**

The candlepower distribution curve shown in option D represents an indirect fixture, which would be a good choice for the classroom. Indirect lighting would illuminate the ceiling and provide even, diffuse light throughout the space without causing glare or reflections on the computer screens.

The candlepower distribution curve shown in option A represents a direct fixture, option B represents a semidirect fixture, and option C represents a semi-indirect fixture.

16.   **The answer is C.**

Incandescent light will make the orange walls appear more vibrant and will provide good color rendering for other colors.

However, incandescent lamps do not have a very long life span and tend not to be as efficient as fluorescent lamps. Warm white fluorescent lamps would be the next best choice, and though their color rendering is not quite as accurate, the owner might select them over the incandescent lamps when other factors are taken into consideration.

Both daylight and cool white fluorescent lamps tend to make things seem a little bluish. These types of light will give the orange a grayer appearance and would not be good selections for this application.

17.   The answer is B.

Metal halide lamps are particularly sensitive to orientation, and they lose efficiency and lumen power if not installed correctly. All metal halide lamps are designated with a proper burning position: base-up, base-down, horizontal, or universal.

The other types of high intensity discharge or HID lamps do not have this characteristic and can be installed in any orientation.

18.   The answer is A and E.

Electronic ballasts have many advantages over conventional ballasts. Many annoyances associated with fluorescent lamps, such as humming and flickering, are greatly reduced or eliminated with electronic ballasts. Electronic ballasts permit lamps to be operated at a wider range of temperatures—down to about 0°F (−18°C)—and let lamps be dimmed more easily and economically. In addition, the ballast itself is smaller and lighter in weight and more energy efficient. Existing fixtures with conventional ballasts can be retrofitted with electronic ballasts to realize the advantages of newer technology.

19.   The answer is D.

Of the four types of lamps listed, the high-pressure sodium lamp generally has the longest life span. A high-pressure sodium bulb can be expected to last around 24,000 hr. A mercury vapor lamp would have a similar life expectancy.

The lamp with the shortest life span is the incandescent bulb. It can be expected to last only about 2000 hr.

The life span of a fluorescent lamp depends on the way the lamp is operated. The life span is affected not only by how many hours the lamp is on but by how many times the lamp is turned on and off. With typical usage patterns, a life span of about 10,000 hr to 20,000 hr can be expected, depending on the type of lamp and ballast used. Depending on the wattage, a metal halide lamp could also be expected to last from 10,000 hr to 20,000 hr.

20.   The answer is A.

Only CPVC (chlorinated polyvinyl chloride) plastic pipe is suitable for use for both hot and cold water supply lines. This type of pipe is also sometimes referred to as PVDC, or polyvinyl dichloride. Because it does not support combustion, it may be used as an alternative to metal piping in some sprinkler systems as local codes permit.

ABS (acrylonitrile butadiene styrene) is rigid, black pipe that is typically used for drainage lines. It is resistant to household chemicals such as laundry detergents, toilet bowl cleaners, and dishwashing soaps.

PVC (polyvinyl chloride) and PE (polyethylene) are acceptable for use as cold water supply lines where they are permitted by local building codes.

PVC pipe can be used for potable water distribution, for waste pipes, and as conduit. PVC pipe is available in different colors depending on its intended use: white, blue, or gray is generally for cold water supply lines, and green is for sewer service. PVC pipe should never be used to transmit compressed gases. It degrades with exposure to ultraviolet radiation, so when used where it will be exposed to sunlight it must be treated for UV resistance and coated with latex paint.

PE pipe can be used for potable water or natural gas distribution, sprinkler systems, and waste lines. A significant advantage to PE pipe is its resistance to becoming brittle in cold temperatures, so it is an excellent choice for exterior applications.

21.   The answer is B.

In a cold climate, it is important to maximize exposure and warming effects of the sun while shielding the building from cold winter winds. Locating the building near the bottom of the slope would provide protection from the wind and exposure to the sun, and lifting the building to a higher elevation would avoid the effects of cold air collecting in the valley.

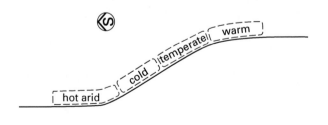

22. The answer is C.

Upfeed water supply systems will work in buildings up to approximately 40 ft to 60 ft (12 m to 18 m) tall, so the most appropriate choice of the selections given is option C, 50 ft to 60 ft (15 m to 18 m). The exact height depends on a variety of factors, including losses due to static head as well as the pressure at the water main, which is generally anywhere from 40 psi to 80 psi (275 kPa to 550 kPa).

Static head is the amount of pressure required to lift water through a piping system in a building. 0.433 psi can lift water 1 ft (10 kPa can lift water 1 m). For each foot (meter) of building height, then, 0.433 psi (10 kPa) is lost. To determine water pressure at each floor of the building, multiply the static head by the building height and subtract this from the pressure at the building main. There must be enough pressure available to operate fixtures on the top floor. These calculations can help a designer to determine the most appropriate type of system for a project.

23. The answer is D.

Cast-iron pipe is typically used for sanitary lines in nonresidential buildings. It is noncorrosive in most soils and resists abrasion from waste materials that may be drained through the pipe as well as from rock and soil on the outside of the pipe in underground installations. Cast-iron pipe is quick to install, readily available, and economical. Because of the thickness of the material and the way that it is joined, cast-iron pipe typically muffles sound.

PVC pipe is a white plastic pipe often used for cold water supply lines. PVC pipe is another option for sanitary lines. It is typically less expensive and easier to install, but it cannot be used for exterior applications or where noise reduction is a consideration.

Copper pipe is generally used for supply lines. ABS is a rigid black plastic pipe used primarily for drainage lines in residential buildings.

24. The answer is B.

120/208 voltage, three-phase power would be appropriate for a small commercial building.

Residences typically have 120/240 voltage, single-phase systems. Larger buildings with greater demand require higher-voltage, three-phase services.

25. The answer is B.

A sound intensity level of 120 dB is almost deafening and can be felt throughout a listener's body. It can cause ringing in the ears and a temporary loss of hearing. Hearing protection should be worn during prolonged exposure to sound intensity levels this high.

Common sound intensity levels range from 0 dB, the threshold of hearing, through 130 dB, the threshold of pain.

26. The answer is B.

Degree days are calculated by comparing the base temperature—in this case, 65°F (18°C)—to the average temperature on a specific date in a specific location. If the day's average temperature is less than 65°F (18°C), subtract the average temperature from the base temperature to determine the number of *heating degree days*; each degree of difference is equivalent to one degree day. If the temperature is above 65°F (18°C), the quantity of heating degree days is 0; however, temperatures above 65°F (18°C) are recorded as *cooling degree days*. If the temperature is 65°F (18°C), no degree days are recorded for that date. To determine the number of degree days in a specified period of time, simply add the number of degree days recorded for each date.

This question asks specifically for heating degree days, which are calculated as follows.

date	heating degree days (°F (°C))
3/1	65 − 41 = 24 (18 − 5 = 13)
3/2	65 − 59 = 6 (18 − 15 = 3)
3/3	65 − 43 = 22 (18 − 6 = 12)
3/4	65 − 42 = 23 (18 − 5 = 13)
3/5	65 − 44 = 21 (18 − 6 = 12)
3/6	65 − 41 = 24 (18 − 5 = 13)
3/7	65 − 39 = 26 (18 − 4 = 14)
3/8	65 − 40 = 25 (18 − 4 = 14)
3/9	65 − 60 = 5 (18 − 15 = 3)
3/10	65 − 70 = 0 (18 − 21 = 0)
3/11	65 − 61 = 4 (18 − 16 = 2)
3/12	65 − 62 = 3 (18 − 17 = 1)
3/13	65 − 65 = 0 (18 − 8 = 0)
3/14	65 − 62 = 3 (18 − 16 = 2)
total	186 (102)

27.   The answer is C.

Hot and cool air are both constantly available in a dual duct system; it can provide heating and cooling simultaneously. (A multizone system also has the capability.) However, the dual duct system has some drawbacks: It is relatively expensive, requires a lot of ductwork (two runs to each space), and is not very energy efficient. Direct expansion, variable air volume, and reheat systems provide heating and cooling but cannot do both at the same time.

28.   The answer is D.

The *building energy cost method* allows the designer to compare the annual energy costs of the design building to a baseline building. If the design energy costs are less in the design building, the building complies with the standard. This method must be used to obtain LEED credit. It cannot be used to analyze a building that does not have a mechanical system.

Two alternative approaches to analyzing annual energy costs are the *system performance method* and the *prescriptive criteria method*. The system performance method requires complex calculations based upon the site's climate. A computer model of the design building is often necessary to complete these calculations. The prescriptive criteria method allows calculations to be completed relatively quickly but tends to be more restrictive than the other methods.

29.   The answer is 10 years.

First calculate the initial (simple) rate of return.

$$\text{initial rate of return} = \frac{\text{annual savings}}{\text{investment}}$$

$$= \frac{\left(\dfrac{\$460}{\text{mo}}\right)\left(12\,\dfrac{\text{mo}}{\text{yr}}\right)}{\$55{,}000}$$

$$= 0.1003/\text{yr} \quad (10.03\%/\text{yr})$$

The simple payback period is the reciprocal of the initial rate of return.

$$\text{simple payback period} = \frac{1}{\text{initial rate of return}}$$

$$= \frac{1}{\dfrac{0.1003}{\text{yr}}}$$

$$= 10\ \text{yr}$$

Although the simple rate of return and payback period are quickly calculated and can be used as a rough guideline, actual rate of return and discounted payback period calculations are much more valuable when assessing the return on investment and comparing alternative systems.

30.   The answer is D.

An STC rating of 40 to 45 would provide the desired sound level on the opposite side of the partition.

31.   The answer is B.

A material's absorption, A, is equivalent to its area, S, multiplied by its coefficient of absorption, α. For convenience, the noise reduction coefficient, NRC, is used for the coefficient of absorption. The total absorption of the room is equivalent to the sum of all materials' absorptions.

$$A_{\text{material}} = S\alpha$$

$$A_{\text{total}} = S_1\alpha_1 + S_2\alpha_2 + S_3\alpha_3 \ldots$$

When calculating the area of the walls, remember to subtract the area of the windows.

In U.S. units:

The total area of the walls (including the windows) is

$$S_{\text{total}} = 2S_{12\,\text{ft}} + 2S_{15\,\text{ft}}$$

$$= (2)(12\ \text{ft})(9\ \text{ft}) + (2)(15\ \text{ft})(9\ \text{ft})$$

$$= 486\ \text{ft}^2$$

The area of the walls without the four windows is

$$S_{\text{walls}} = S_{\text{total}} - 4S_{\text{window}}$$

$$= 486\ \text{ft}^2 - (4)(5\ \text{ft})(3\ \text{ft})$$

$$= 426\ \text{ft}^2$$

The absorptions of the materials in the office are

$$A = S\alpha$$

$$A_{\text{walls}} = (426\ \text{ft}^2)(0.05) = 21.3\ \text{sabins (ft}^2)$$

$$A_{\text{ceiling}} = (12\ \text{ft})(15\ \text{ft})(0.60) = 108\ \text{sabins (ft}^2)$$

$$A_{\text{floor}} = (12\ \text{ft})(15\ \text{ft})(0.55) = 99\ \text{sabins (ft}^2)$$

$$A_{\text{windows}} = (4)(5\ \text{ft})(3\ \text{ft})(0.15) = 9\ \text{sabins (ft}^2)$$

The total absorption is the sum of these, or 237.3 sabins (ft²).

In SI units:

The total area of the walls (including the windows) is

$$S_{total} = 2S_{4\,m} + 2S_{5\,m}$$
$$= (2)(4\text{ m})(3\text{ m}) + (2)(5\text{ m})(3\text{ m})$$
$$= 54\text{ m}^2$$

The area of the walls without the four windows is

$$S_{walls} = S_{total} - 4S_{window}$$
$$= 54\text{ m}^2 - (4)(1.5\text{ m})(1\text{ m})$$
$$= 48\text{ m}^2$$

The absorptions of the materials in the office are

$$A = S\alpha$$
$$A_{walls} = (48\text{ m}^2)(0.05) = 2.4\text{ sabins (m}^2)$$
$$A_{ceiling} = (4\text{ m})(5\text{ m})(0.60) = 12\text{ sabins (m}^2)$$
$$A_{floor} = (4\text{ m})(5\text{ m})(0.55) = 11\text{ sabins (m}^2)$$
$$A_{windows} = (4)(1.5\text{ m})(1\text{ m})(0.15) = 0.9\text{ sabins (m}^2)$$

The total absorption is the sum of these, or 26.3 sabins (m²).

32. The answer is B.

The minimum width of the lobby should be 10 ft (3.0 m). As a general rule, it is most economical and efficient to group elevators into "banks." A 10 ft (3.0 m) wide lobby will allow sufficient space for a group of passengers to gather, but is small enough that a person in the lobby can see all of the elevators while waiting for an available car.

33. The answer is B.

Buildings that are well-sealed use energy more efficiently. All of the pieces of equipment listed are diagnostic tools used to measure how well a building is sealed, to quantify how much air is leaking in or out, and to identify the locations of leaks.

A *blower door* is a fan that can be mounted in a door frame. It is used to pressurize or depressurize a building to measure air infiltration or leakage.

A *nanometer* measures differences in pressure between two spaces. A *flow hood* is placed over a register or diffuser to measure output. A *duct blower* is similar to a blower door, but it is attached directly to the ductwork to check for leaks.

34. The answer is A.

Flexible metal conduit should be used to connect to a motor because it can "give" with the movement of the machinery. It is a good choice for any location where there is vibration or where it is impossible to use a straight run of rigid conduit.

35. The answer is D.

The system shown in the diagram is a 120/208 voltage, three-phase, four-wire electrical system. Taps that connect to a hot wire and a neutral wire produce 120 V service (such as at convenience receptacles); *a* and *b* are 120 V taps. Taps that connect to two hot wires produce 208 V service; *c* and *d* are 208 V taps.

120/240 V power is produced by a single-phase, three-wire system. It is found primarily in residences, with the 120 V power directed to convenience receptacles and light fixtures and the 240 V reserved for equipment such as air conditioners or clothes dryers. 277/480 V power systems are diagrammatically similar to the 120/208 V system shown, but step-down transformers are required to convert the higher voltages to 120 V for receptacles.

36. The answer is C.

A *variable air volume* (VAV) system would be the best choice for this application. VAV systems allow for maximum individual control of temperature, quiet operation, and minimal maintenance.

Packaged terminal units and *fan coil terminals* permit control over the temperatures of individual spaces but do not operate as quietly or require as little maintenance as VAV systems.

Single duct, constant air volume (CAV) units are relatively inexpensive to install and maintain but do not offer occupants the ability to control the temperatures of individual spaces.

37.   The answer is A.

A person standing along the marble wall near the entrance to Union Station and who is speaking softly can be heard clearly from across the lobby. The arch works because the sound is *focused* by the concave surfaces and directed into a specific part of the room—in this case, the niche on the other side of the lobby.

Creep is the reflection of sound along a curved surface, such as a dome. The sound can be understood at points along the way but cannot be heard across the room. *Diffusion* is the opposite of focusing, where sound is scattered all around a room as it is reflected from convex surfaces. *Specular reflection* is the reflection of sound off hard, polished surfaces.

38.   The answer is A.

Symbol I is a computer data outlet. A variation of this symbol is to include a plus sign at the left side and draw the symbol with a point of the triangle at the outlet's location on the wall. If the triangle were not shaded, the symbol would represent a telephone outlet.

Symbol II is a duplex floor receptacle. Most types of receptacles can be placed in the floor as long as a protective covering is provided to prevent loose objects, dirt, water, or cleaning products from entering the receptacle. The square around the duplex receptacle symbol indicates that it is located in the floor.

Symbol III is a home run to a panel board. The number of arrows should correspond to the number of circuits. If arrows are not shown, it is assumed to be a two-wire circuit.

Symbol IV is an exit sign. The shaded areas of the symbol represent the faces of the sign. This particular symbol indicates an exit sign that is ceiling-mounted and both sides of the sign are visible. If it were a wall-mounted sign, it would have one face and only one quarter of the symbol would be shaded.

A key to common electrical symbols can be found in *Architectural Graphic Standards* and in the Construction Specification Institute's *Uniform Drawing System*. The symbols depicted in this question are those used by CSI.

39.   The answer is B.

This problem can be solved using the basic definition of energy: energy equals power multiplied by time ($E = Pt$). To wash and dry four loads of laundry, the washer will be in use for 3 hr (4 loads times 0.75 hr/load) and the dryer will be running for 4 hr (4 loads times 1 hr/load).

$$E = Pt$$
$$E_{washer} = (750\ \text{W})\left(\frac{1\ \text{kW}}{1000\ \text{W}}\right)(3\ \text{hr})$$
$$= 2.25\ \text{kW-hr}$$
$$E_{dryer} = (5000\ \text{W})\left(\frac{1\ \text{kW}}{1000\ \text{W}}\right)(4\ \text{hr})$$
$$= 20.0\ \text{kW-hr}$$
$$E_{iron} = (800\ \text{W})\left(\frac{1\ \text{kW}}{1000\ \text{W}}\right)(1\ \text{hr})$$
$$= 0.80\ \text{kW-hr}$$
$$E_{total} = E_{washer} + E_{dryer} + E_{iron}$$
$$= 2.25\ \text{kW-hr} + 20.0\ \text{kW-hr}$$
$$+ 0.80\ \text{kW-hr}$$
$$= 23.05\ \text{kW-hr}$$
$$\text{cost} = E_{total}(\text{rate})$$
$$= (23.05\ \text{kW-hr})\left(\frac{\$0.08}{\text{kW-hr}}\right)$$
$$= \$1.84$$

40.   The answer is D.

Aluminum conduit should not be used in concrete slabs because it tends to cause spalling and cracking if it reacts with ingredients in the concrete admixtures.

Many of the rules for placing conduit in concrete slabs are similar to those for reinforcing bars. Conduit should always be placed in the part of the slab that is in tension. It is important to cover the conduit with at least $^3/_4$ in (19) of concrete, and in locations where heavy loads will be applied to the slab, the coating should be even thicker. The designer must take care to specify conduit of an appropriate size relative to the thickness of the slab. The outside diameter of the conduit should be no greater than $^1/_3$ of the slab thickness. It is also important to allow an adequate amount of space between parallel runs of conduit—at least three times the outside diameter of the largest tube.

41.   The answer is B and C.

Generally, spaces intended to highlight spoken-word presentations should be "dead" spaces; that is, they should have short reverberation times. Musical presentations generally sound best in spaces with long reverberation times, or spaces that are "live."

Reverberation time is calculated as

$$T_R = \frac{0.049V}{A}$$

V equals the volume of the space, and A equals total absorptivity of the wall, floor, and ceiling surfaces along with other absorptive elements, such as upholstered seats, curtains, and so on. When a program or occupancy dictates the size of the room, dead spaces can often be created by specifying absorptive materials and live spaces can be created by using materials that reflect sound.

42. The answer is B.

The *stack vent* is the portion of the soil stack above the highest plumbing fixture. It serves as a vent for the stack and is open to the outside at the top. A *vent stack* is a collection of vents from a number of fixtures that share one exterior outlet. A *cleanout* is an area of the plumbing that can be accessed to clear obstructions from the system. A *vacuum breaker* is a flap that opens to admit air if there is suction in a water pipe, which prevents siphoning of wastewater back into the clean water supply system.

43. The answer is A, C, and F.

Fire extinguishers should always be available in buildings to combat a fire as quickly as possible. They should be located a maximum of 75 ft (23 m) from every building occupant or as required by local building codes. *Wet standpipes* may also be available for building occupants' use. They consist of a large pipe running vertically through a building and connected to at least one hose on each floor (the exact number of hoses is determined by building layout and local codes). The occupants can access the hose and release the water as necessary. *Two-way communications devices* are installed for building occupants' use so that those who are having difficulty evacuating the building may call for help.

Dry standpipes must be connected to a pumper truck in order to be filled with water. They are designed to be used by the fire department to distribute water throughout a building. The firefighters enter the building and attach their hoses to the standpipe outlets on each floor to fight the fire.

A *fusible link* is a sensor in a sprinkler head and is not activated by building occupants but rather by a rise in ambient temperature indicating the presence of fire. *Annunciators* are used to give instructions to building occupants. They are used by firefighters or others authorized to assist with evacuation efforts.

44. The answer is B.

A sound composed of a single frequency is called a *tone*.

A *chord* is a combination of notes played simultaneously.

Sound waves can be represented by a sine curve. A *note* represents a specific frequency of wavelength. The *pitch* is the number of complete wave forms per second.

45. The answer is C.

Class C fire extinguishers are for electrical fires. They contain an extinguishing chemical, often Halon or carbon dioxide, that will not conduct electricity. After the electricity has been disconnected, Class A or B fire extinguishers may be used on a fire that was originally electrical in nature. Class C fire extinguishers are marked with an illustration of a flaming electrical receptacle and a plug. (In the former labeling system, they were marked with a blue circle and the letter C.)

Class A fire extinguishers are for ordinary combustible materials such as paper or wood and usually use water or a dry chemical as the extinguishing agent. They are marked with an illustration of a burning stack of firewood and a trash can. (Older models may be marked with a green triangle and the letter A.) Class B extinguishers are for flammable gases and are marked with an illustration of a flaming can of gasoline. (The older labeling system marks them with a red square and the letter B.) Class D extinguishers are for combustible metals and are not marked with an illustration. Multi-class extinguishers are available that can be used for a variety of types of fires.

Fire extinguishers are covered in depth in NFPA 10: *Standard for Portable Fire Extinguishers*.

46. The answer is D.

$q_c = UA\Delta T$ is the formula for conduction and is a factor in determining total heating load.

The equation used to calculate total cooling load is

$$q_{total} = q_p + q_m + q_l + q_{CLTD} + q_r$$

Each of the other equations is a factor in calculating cooling load because they each represent internal heat gains.

$q_r = (SG)(SC)A$ is the formula for calculating *insolation*, or total radiant heat gain, through windows (r identifies radiant).

$q_m = 1500(BHP)$ allows the designer to calculate heat gain from equipment (m identifies mechanical).

$q_{CLTD} = UA(CLTD)$ represents the cooling load temperature differential, which allows calculation of heat gain through walls.

Other factors in determining cooling load are q_p, which quantifies heat gain from building occupants (p identifies people), and q_l, which is a calculation of heat gain from lighting fixtures (l identifies lighting).

47.   The answer is B.

Electric baseboard heaters transfer heat through convection. The air in contact with the heater at the floor becomes warmer and rises. Then, the cooler air in the upper part of the room falls and is heated by the baseboard heaters, and it rises. The process continues and convective currents move through the space, bringing the air to a constant temperature.

48.   The answer is B.

Although incandescent lamp shapes are often referred to only by their letter designation, it is helpful to know the descriptions that the letters represent.

A	arbitrary (standard shape)
PS	pear shape, straight neck
P	pear shape
S	straight
G	globe
T	tubular
PAR	parabolic aluminized reflector
R	reflector
ER	elliptical reflector
MR	miniature reflector

49.   The answer is C.

Decibel levels are expressed on a logarithmic scale and cannot be simply added together (i.e., 90 dB + 95 dB ≠ 185 dB). It is necessary to examine the difference between the two decibel levels and add an appropriate factor to the larger level. In this case, the difference is 5, so according to the following table, 1.2 should be added to 95, the larger level.

Use the following table for adding decibel levels.

difference in dB level	add to the larger dB level
0	3.0
1	2.5
2	2.1
3	1.8
4	1.5
5	1.2
6	1.0
7	0.8
8	0.6
9	0.5
10	0.4

50.   The answer is C, E, and F.

Areas of positive pressure would occur on the windward side of the building as the wind pushes against the building wall. Areas of negative pressure occur on the sides of the building and on the leeward side. Because the building in the diagram has no fenestration, the pressure inside the building would be neutral.

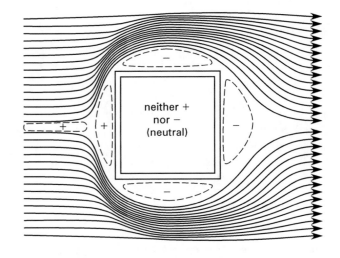

Used with permission from Fuller Moore, Environmental Control Systems: Heating Cooling Lighting, copyright © 2004, by Fuller Moore.

51.   The answer is A.

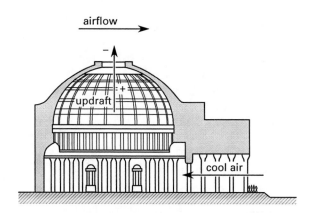

The Pantheon is naturally cooled through *stack ventilation*. Cool air is drawn into the building through the portico and travels through the drum to cool the interior space before being vented through the oculus at the top of the dome. Wind flowing over the top of the building creates negative pressure that sucks the air through the building, so the system is effective regardless of the direction of the wind.

The other three options are also natural cooling techniques. *Pools of water* can be placed in courtyards or near building openings in hot, arid climates to cool the air entering the interior spaces through evaporation.

In the *thermal mass* strategy of natural cooling, heat is stored during the day and the building is opened for ventilation at night. The mass is cooled and ready to absorb heat the next day.

Placing openings on parallel walls and orienting them to the prevailing winds creates *cross ventilation* and increases the velocity of the air moving through a space. This is an effective cooling technique for hot, humid climates.

52.   The answer is A.

The primary determinants of thermal comfort are

- air temperature
- humidity
- surface temperature
- air motion
- activity level
- clothing

While a designer can control the first four, the building occupants control what they do and what they wear.

It is popularly believed that factors such as age, nationality, gender, and body build can influence levels of thermal comfort, but it has been proven that they have little to no effect.

53.   The answer is D.

The house depicted would be appropriate for a temperate climate, such as that of Maryland. The longest facade is oriented east-west, exposing most windows to the south to take advantage of winter sun. The porch on the south side shades the first-floor windows in the summer, as does the deciduous tree to the south, which blocks the sun's rays in the hottest months and allows the sun to shine through during the winter when the tree is bare. Sometimes evergreen trees are planted to the north to block the winter winds. The heat source (fireplace) is located at the end of the building, and the kitchen is located to the north since it will create its own heat.

54.   The answer is B.

Specific heat is the amount of heat in Btu required to raise the temperature of one unit of mass one degree of temperature. This value is directly related to thermal storage capacity. The specific heat of water is the value against which all other materials are measured. Water has nearly five times the thermal storage capacity of concrete, more than three times the thermal storage capacity of adobe, and about one and a half times the thermal storage capacity of gypsum.

55.   The answer is C.

If an elevator should begin traveling excessively fast, the first safety device to activate is the *centrifugal governor*, which sets the brake and shuts off the power. If that does not stop the car, the *safety rail clamps* wedge against the guide rails and stop the car smoothly. *Final-limit switches* are activated if the elevator overruns the safe limits of travel either up or down. *Buffers* are installed in the elevator pit to cushion the elevator as it stops, but they are not capable of stopping a falling car.

56.   The answer is A and B.

Because of their ability to deplete the earth's ozone layer, the production of certain refrigerants has been discontinued in the United States in compliance with the Montreal Protocol on Substances that Deplete the Ozone Layer. Halon production ceased in 1994. U.S. production of CFCs stopped in 1995. HFCs will continue to be produced, but they are not without their own environmental challenges, as they have a high global warming potential. HCFCs will be phased out by 2030.

More information about ozone-depleting substances can be found on the Environmental Protection Agency's website, epa.gov/ozone.

57.   The answer is C.

The uppermost curved line on the psychrometric chart represents 100% relative humidity, or fully saturated air. This is also known as the *dew point*, because it is the temperature at which water in the air begins to condense on surfaces.

58.   The answer is B.

The range receptacle is pictured in option B. Option A is an air conditioning receptacle, option C is a dryer receptacle, and option D is a standard three-prong receptacle.

59.   The answer is C.

Escalators typically travel at a speed of 100 ft/min (30 m/min). Both the handrail and steps must travel at exactly the same speed.

60.   The answer is D.

Escalators are always installed at an angle of 30° from horizontal. All of the other statements are false. An escalator can never be counted as a means of egress because it is unprotected. Structural support is required only at the top and the bottom of the escalator, the points upon which the truss structure underneath the moving steps bears. Emergency power is rarely required for escalators since it is basically impossible to become trapped on one; a passenger could climb up or down the stopped stairs to evacuate.

61.   The answer is D.

Planting a combination of deciduous and evergreen trees is the most effective sound attenuation strategy. Planting the trees on an earth mound would further improve the effectiveness of the buffer.

62.   The answer is 16 water closets.

This problem asks only for a calculation of water closets, so the information on lavatories, urinals, and drinking fountains can be disregarded.

$$\frac{400 \text{ girls}}{35 \dfrac{\text{girls}}{\text{water closet}}} = 11.42 \text{ girls' water closets}$$

$$\frac{350 \text{ boys}}{100 \dfrac{\text{boys}}{\text{water closet}}} = 3.50 \text{ boys' water closets}$$

Toilet fixture calculations are always rounded up, so 12 girls' and 4 boys' water closets are needed.

63.   The answer is B.

A *brightness ratio* is the relationship between the illumination levels of the surfaces within a person's field of vision. The maximum ideal brightness level ratio between a task and the adjacent surroundings should be under $1{:}^{1}/_{3}$.

64.   The answer is D.

Values in the zone indicated on the chart necessitate *humidification*, or adding moisture to the air, to prevent static electricity, uncomfortable breathing, and the potential for nosebleeds and dry skin. Humidification can be accomplished either with a central humidification system at the HVAC unit, which treats the air before it is distributed throughout the building or, in smaller buildings or residences, with point-of-use humidifiers.

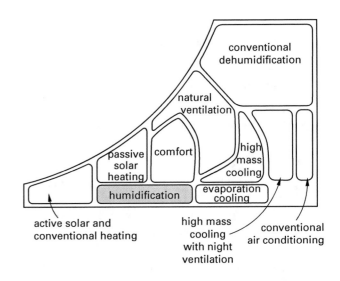

This *extremely* simplified diagram of the psychrometric chart provides a quick reference to the best approaches for each region of the chart. Note that they are not the only strategies that will work for a specific reading, and that the areas of the chart where the strategy can be successful overlap more than this diagram implies. A more detailed chart that illustrates the overlap can be found in *Mechanical and Electrical Equipment for Buildings*, by Stein and others.

65.   The answer is A.

Forced air systems occupy the most space within the building because of the size of the mechanical unit itself and the amount of ductwork necessary to distribute the conditioned air.

66.   The answer is B.

The ceiling height is not a contributing factor in zonal cavity method calculations. The zonal cavity method allows a designer to calculate the number of fixtures required to produce a specified number of footcandles.

The zonal cavity method equation is

$$E = \frac{Nn(\text{LL})(\text{LLD})(\text{DDF})(\text{CU})}{A}$$

E = illumination in footcandles

N = number of fixtures

n = number of lamps

LL = lumens per lamp

LLD = lamp lumen depreciation factor

DDF = dirt depreciation factor

CU = coefficient of utilization

A = area of the space

67.   The answer is B.

Power (P) is a function of voltage (V), current (I), and the power factor (PF).

$$P = VI(\text{PF})\sqrt{3}$$
$$= (208 \text{ V})(9 \text{ A})(0.75)\sqrt{3}$$
$$= 2428.92 \text{ W} \quad (2.4 \text{ kW})$$

68.   The answer is C.

A *submersible pump* is commonly used for small buildings and residences with a private water supply from a well. The pump is placed below the water table and pumps the water from the well to a pressure tank.

Suction pumps work best in very shallow wells (less than 25 ft (7.6 m) in depth). *Jet pumps*, also called *venturi pumps*, force water to the surface via the venturi principle, which uses differences in water pressure to move the water up. They are good for wells that are from 25 ft (7.6 m) to more

than 100 ft (30.5 m) deep. *Turbine pumps* are designed for very deep wells with high capacity.

69.   The answer is C.

The *vertical displacement ventilation* approach (sometimes called *thermal displacement ventilation*) to HVAC design differs markedly from the traditional forced air approach. It relies on the difference in density between "zones" or strata in the space. It is often used in classroom environments because it is not noisy or disruptive, it provides excellent ventilation of contaminants such as the carbon dioxide emitted from large assemblies of students, and it improves indoor air quality while being energy efficient.

Rather than delivering cold supply air at high velocities like a conventional mixing system, displacement ventilation provides cool supply air at low velocities near the floor. The air in the conditioned space is not mixed but remains stratified, with the cooler air near the floor and the warmer air near the ceiling. Because the air is delivered at low velocities, drafts in the space are eliminated and the system is much quieter because the fans do not need to operate at high speeds. As the air warms up through contact with building occupants, it rises to the ceiling. Carbon dioxide and other contaminants are whisked to the top of the space along with the warm air. The contaminated, warm air is exhausted at the ceiling. Because the air is not mixed throughout the room and the heat produced by light fixtures remains near the top of the space, less cooling capacity is required to keep the occupants comfortable.

A design brief discussing displacement ventilation can be downloaded from the Energy Design Resources' website, www.energydesignresources.com. A link to the brief can be found at **www.ppi2pass.com/resources**.

70.   The answer is C.

Demand-controlled ventilation (DCV) technology uses a carbon dioxide sensor to increase or decrease ventilation of a space according to occupancy. This technology is best used for spaces where the occupancy of the space can vary greatly at different times during the day or week and where there is not a high concentration of air contaminants that need to be exhausted through a continuously operating HVAC system. A bowling alley would be a good application of DCV because it has long operating hours but widely varying occupancy levels. Although the bowling alley may be open during the afternoon during the week, there probably would not be as many people present then as there would be on a Friday or Saturday night. A DCV system would increase ventilation of the space when necessary and decrease it when the building is less full.

DCV technology is not a good choice for spaces where there are odors or contaminants that must be constantly exhausted or for spaces that are always occupied. Therefore, the pet store, the locker room, and the dry cleaner would not be good applications of this technology because there are air quality issues to be addressed beyond those determined by occupancy.

Demand-controlled ventilation is a relatively new technology. A good primer on its best applications and potential cost savings is available from E Source, a clearinghouse of energy information. A link can be found at **www.ppi2pass.com/resources**.

71. The answer is A.

Photoelectric cells are a type of perimeter security system. Perimeter systems secure building entry points such as doors and windows. Photoelectric cells pass a beam from one point to another and sound an alarm when the beam is broken.

The other three types of security systems are area or room protection systems. They sense when an intruder is in a protected room and sound an alarm. *Pressure sensors* detect changes in pressure on the floor caused by a person walking. *Ultrasonic detectors* use a high-frequency sound wave to sense intruders. *Photoelectric beams* use infrared technology to protect a space. If the photoelectric beam is broken by an intruder's movements, an alarm sounds.

72. The answer is 13.

The minimum *seasonal energy efficiency ratio* (SEER) for all residential air conditioning equipment manufactured in the United States is 13. This is an increase from the previous minimum rating of 10, so the new rating represents approximately a 30% improvement in energy efficiency.

73. The answer is C.

Transformer specifications should include the type of transformer, phase, voltage, kVA (kilovolt-ampere) rating, sound level, and insulation class.

It is unlikely that the physical dimensions of a transformer would be included in the specification, as the size tends to be determined by the technical criteria, particularly by the capacity and insulation type. The size of units can vary greatly from one manufacturer to the next.

74. The answer is C.

The receptacle in the finished living area of a basement would not be required to be GFCI-protected because it is not located in an exterior space, in a space that could potentially be damp (such as a crawlspace), or in a place where water will be present.

GFCI, or *ground fault circuit interrupter*, protection is available on both receptacles and breakers. The devices constantly monitor the amount of electricity flowing through the circuit. If the GFCI detects any variation, indicating that there is a "leak" and current is flowing out of the circuit and into the ground (potentially through a person), it instantly shuts off the power to that circuit. The person may still be shocked but will not be electrocuted.

75. The answer is A.

According to the National Fire Protection Association (NFPA), installing a sprinkler system in a new building adds about 1% to 1.5% to the total construction cost. Retrofitting an existing structure costs considerably more. Sprinkler systems can reduce the risk of death and property loss by one-half to two-thirds, and they are encouraged, if not required, in all types of buildings, including single-family residences, where more than 80% of fire deaths occur.

76. The answer is D.

It is best not to put all of the fixtures and receptacles in a room on the same circuit, although this is sometimes done in very small rooms. The recommendation is to use at least two circuits so that if the breaker is tripped, there will still be some light available to go to the panel box to fix the breaker.

77. The answer is A.

Selective collective operation is a good choice for the apartment building. It collects calls and answers the up calls on the up trip, travels to the floor level with the highest call, then collects and answers the down calls on the return trip to the floor level with the lowest call. This type of operating system works best with more than one car, because cars can be making separate trips and answering calls simultaneously, reducing waiting time at the stops.

Computerized controls are much more sophisticated (and more expensive) than the other three types. They are programmed based on data about building traffic patterns and analysis of the most important calls. *Single automatic control* answers one call at a time, delivers that passenger to the destination, and then responds to the next call. *Collective control* answers all calls without differentiating between up and down calls, so waiting time and time spent on the elevator can be unacceptably long. This type of system is rarely used in new projects in the United States.

78. The answer is C.

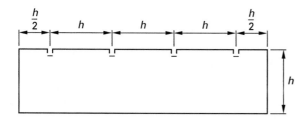

A good guideline for the initial layout of ceiling diffusers in a room is to space them approximately the same distance apart as the room is high. The height of the room is considered to be the distance from the floor to the nearest ceiling element. Diffusers at the edge of the space should be placed about half that distance from the perimeter walls.

79. The answer is C.

Hot water and drain pipes must be protected with an enclosure or wrapped with insulation or plastic covers so that a handicapped person cannot come in contact with them and be burned. The plumbing is not required to be concealed within cabinetry.

The *ADA/ABA Guidelines* require the following for accessible lavatories. (Note that some of these guidelines are different for lavatories designed primarily for children's use. Review the *ADA/ABA Guidelines* for more information.)

- The rim of the lavatory should be no higher than 34 in (865) above the finish floor.
- There should be an apron clearance of at least 29 in (735).
- There must be 30 in (760) by 48 in (1220) area of clear floor space for forward approach extending a maximum of 19 in (485) under the lavatory. This clear floor space must adjoin or overlap an accessible route.
- Each sink shall be a maximum of 6$\frac{1}{2}$ in (165) deep.
- All plumbing pipes are to be insulated or otherwise protected against contact, with no sharp or rough edges under the sink.

The *ADA/ABA Guidelines* can be reviewed at the following link: www.access-board.gov. A link can also be found at **www.ppi2pass.com/AREresources.**

80. The answer is C.

A *curtain board*, also called a *draft curtain*, is an assembly suspended from the ceiling to prohibit movement of smoke and flame. Since smoke rises and gathers at the ceiling, the curtain board helps to block it from entering an adjacent space. Curtain boards are often used to protect openings in the floor, such as escalators and mezzanines. The depth of the curtain board varies and must be confirmed for a specific project.

81. The answer is B.

Fixture units are a measurement of the amount of water required to operate a plumbing fixture. The fixture units assigned to each fixture in a building can be added to determine that building's total demand and to size plumbing pipes.

A flush-valve water closet demands the most water of the four fixtures listed: 10 fixture units. A flush-tank toilet demands about half that amount. Washing machines can demand anywhere from 1.4 to 3 fixture units, depending on the capacity and type of machine. Lavatories demand just 2 fixture units.

Fixture unit values can be determined using charts from the *International Plumbing Code* or similar codes in effect in local jurisdictions.

82. The answer is B.

There are three types of photovoltaic (PV) cells: crystalline, polycrystalline, and amorphous (also known as thin-film). Crystalline cells are the best power generators. They also tend to be the most expensive. Polycrystalline cells produce less power but are more competitively priced. Amorphous PV cells produce the least power, but are unique in that they can be applied onto other building materials (such as roofing materials) to capture solar energy with a less obtrusive appearance.

83. The answer is C.

Evaporative coolers are only effective in this type of climate, but this is not a passive cooling technique. All the other choices would be good ways to passively cool a building in New Mexico's hot-arid climate. Roof ponds add thermal mass to the building; when used in tandem with high thermal mass building materials and night flushing, it is possible to take advantage of the cool nighttime temperatures. Courtyards help keep cooled air within the living space, and the fountains would cool through evaporation and have a psychological effect of making the space seem cooler.

84.   The answer is B.

Doubling the absorptive surfaces in a room would result in a noise reduction of only 3 dB, which would be barely perceptible. To justify the expense of adding more absorptive materials, the absorption should be tripled. With three times the amount of absorption, the change would be about 5 dB and the level of noise reduction would be clearly noticeable.

85.   The answer is A, B, and D.

Boiler rooms and chilled water plants should be located adjacent to one another when possible; in some buildings, the two functions are placed in the same room. It is imperative that the rooms each have at least one exterior wall to permit access to fuel tanks that may be located outside and to allow for adequate ventilation. Recommended ceiling heights vary depending on the type of equipment chosen, but generally 12 ft (3.7 m) is the minimum. The rooms should be long and narrow rather than square and sized to best accommodate the equipment.

Both boilers and chillers are heavy and require additional structural support. It is often most economical to locate them on the ground floor, but this is not required. They tend to be noisy, so the mechanical rooms should be placed in locations within the building where the noise will not disrupt critical tasks. Soundproofing techniques should also be integrated to acoustically separate the mechanical rooms from the occupied spaces.

86.   The answer is D.

The fixtures shown in this typical restroom layout are all wall-hung, so at least 24 in (610) of clear space should be allowed within the plumbing wall to accommodate the plumbing and the carriers that support the fixtures.

If there were fixtures on only one side of the wall, a 12 in (305) space would be adequate. If the fixtures were not wall-hung (tank-type toilets and pedestal sinks, for example), a 16 in (406) space would be sufficient.

87.   The answer is A, B, D, and F.

Building commissioning can be expected to provide increased energy efficiency, improved indoor air quality, a comprehensive training program (conducted either by the commissioning agent or the contractor), and organized operations and maintenance manuals (assembled by the contractor, design professional, or commissioning agent). Building commissioning does not ensure verification of 100% of building systems (that responsibility lies with the contractor) and does not include record drawings.

Building commissioning is a process that helps to assure that a building owner "gets what he paid for." Commissioning takes place in parallel to the traditional design process. The commissioning agent (sometimes abbreviated as CxA or CXA) is hired by the owner and reports directly to the owner. The commissioning agent's job is to verify that the owner's goals are being accomplished and to advocate for the owner. Sometimes this person is a member of the owner's staff, but often a third-party consultant is hired to fill this role.

The first step is to document the owner's goals, which must be quantifiable. For example, perhaps the owner wishes to improve energy efficiency by 10%, as compared to a "study" building. The CxA can evaluate the systems in comparison to the baseline building to determine whether the design fulfills the owner's expectations.

The commissioning agent should be a part of the project team from the beginning and should have input into the programming phase, review the construction documents and specifications for compliance with the owner's goals, and conduct site checks during construction. The agent is responsible for testing a representative sample of the systems. The presence of a commissioning agent on a project team does not relieve the design professionals of any of their responsibilities; the architect and engineer retain responsibility for the design of the building and its systems, and the contractor holds the responsibility for the installation and full testing of the systems. The commissioning process is a quality control check to ensure that the finished building operates in the way that the owner intended.

At the end of the project, the commissioning agent should prepare a report summarizing the owner's goals, the results of the commissioning agent's evaluations, and any outstanding issues or further testing needed (such as seasonal testing of an HVAC system). Building commissioning is a prerequisite for LEED certification. More information on building commissioning can be found at the Building Commissioning Association's website, www.bcxa.org.

88.   The answer is D.

Electric lighting generally demands half of the total energy consumed by an office building. Heating and cooling systems demand about 30%. The remaining 20% is used to operate equipment in the building (such as copy machines, computers, and so on) and for other uses. Since offices are typically used most heavily during the daytime, a good case can be made for integrating daylighting techniques into the design of the building. Daylighting may also reduce the building's total energy consumption, because the cooling load contributed by the electric lights is greatly reduced.

89. The answer is B.

Fiber optics originally was developed by the telecommunications industry to transmit large amounts of data with cables much smaller and lighter in weight than traditional copper cables. Today, most of the telephone system relies on fiber optic technology, and it has also found great acceptance with cable television and power companies and in local area networks (LANs).

Fiber optics transmits data through light pulses. Each system consists of a transmitter, fiber optic lines, and a receiver. The transmitter interprets the electrical pulse information from copper wires linked to the source and translates it to light-pulse information that will travel through the fiber. At the other end, the receiver interprets the light-pulse information and translates it to electrical-pulse information, which then travels through copper wire again to the telephone, computer, or television.

Fiber optic cables are much lighter in weight than copper wire and can carry much more information. A cable consists of a core that transmits the information, and several layers of claddings and coatings that protect the core. The fibers are classified as either single-mode or multi-mode. In single-mode fibers, the light travels in a straight path; in multi-mode fibers, the light reflects off the interior of the core and travels in a zigzag path. Single-mode fibers can carry more information than multi-mode fibers but are more expensive.

A good online resource for learning more about fiber optics is the "Fiber Optic Cable Tutorial" (www.arcelect.com/fibercable.htm).

90. The answer is D.

Sick building syndrome is a term used to describe conditions where a significant number of building occupants report some type of physical malaise within a specified period of time, usually about two weeks. Physical symptoms can include dizziness, skin irritation, headaches, nausea, sore throats, and other respiratory problems. Generally, these symptoms disappear or are significantly reduced when the occupants leave the building. Occupant complaints are usually the first indicator that there is a problem in the

building, and further testing and inspection is warranted to determine the source of their discomfort.

Sick building syndrome can usually be traced to a few common causes. Insufficient or contaminated outdoor air entering the HVAC system is the most common reason for occupant complaints. This can be caused by improper balancing of the system, or by locating the air intakes too close to a source of contamination such as an exhaust, parking, or trash collection area. Insufficient ventilation of spaces where there is a high concentration of chemicals or contaminants—such as a janitor's closet, smoking area, or a copy room—could be another reason. Occasionally, occupant complaints are linked to mold growth in hidden areas of the building or within the HVAC system. Designing the HVAC system to prevent the accumulation of stagnant water and cleaning the ductwork frequently helps prevent mold growth. Complaints can also arise when materials with high levels of volatile organic compounds (VOCs) are introduced, such as new carpeting or paint. Low-VOC materials should be specified when possible.

It is widely believed that incorporating living plants into a building can alleviate some of the symptoms of sick building syndrome, but this has yet to be determined conclusively. Preliminary research by the National Aeronautics and Space Administration (NASA) seems to indicate that plants filter some contaminants out of indoor air. However, the Environmental Protection Agency (EPA) disagrees, stating that plants do not have a significant effect on indoor air quality and that the NASA research was conducted under laboratory conditions not applicable to real-world scenarios. Even if plants do have some effect, it would be extremely small in comparison to the effectiveness of increasing the quantity and quality of mechanical ventilation.

91. The answer is A.

Nearly 40% of a restaurant's construction budget would be allocated for HVAC. This would include ventilation of the kitchen in addition to multizone climate control for the dining areas.

A hospital's construction budget would include a 20% allowance for HVAC. About 10% of the total construction cost for the climate controlled mini-warehouse would be related to heating, ventilation, and cooling. A typical parking garage would contain no HVAC systems.

More information about typical costs for building construction can be found in the current edition of *Square Foot Costs*, published by R.S. Means, a division of Reed Construction Data, Inc.

92.   The answer is B.

Substation transformers are always mounted on a concrete pad because they tend to be very large. Distribution transformers are smaller in size and can be mounted either on a pole or on a pad.

93.   The answer is B.

For maximum power generation, the photovoltaic (PV) panels should be mounted facing due south, in a location where the panels will not be shaded. The ideal angle depends on the project location, the purpose of the solar collectors, and the time of year; for this reason, it is best to mount them on a moveable frame or use a "tracker" so that their position can be modified. As a general guideline, fixed panels should be mounted at an angle approximately equivalent to the latitude. It is also possible to generate electricity from configurations facing east or west, but north-facing installations are not recommended.

94.   The answer is D.

Wye-to-wye connections are rarely used because they can cause problems with harmonics and can interfere with communications systems within the building.

95.   The answer is A.

The sound intensity level at the back row of the classroom would be 53 dB. Sound intensity levels decrease 6 dB for every doubling of distance. The simple math in this problem makes it easy to solve in this manner, as 3 ft (1 m) doubled is 6 ft (2 m), and 6 ft (2 m) doubled is 12 ft (4 m). The total drop is 12 dB, and 65 dB − 12 dB = 53 dB.

PRACTICE EXAM: VIGNETTE SOLUTION

MECHANICAL AND ELECTRICAL PLAN: PASSING SOLUTION

This vignette requires that the examinee establish a layout for a simple exposed grid acoustical ceiling system, locate lights, and provide a schematic layout for an HVAC system. The lighting layout must be established by using the light distribution diagrams provided.

Solving Approach

Step 1 Lay out the fluorescent light fixture locations, keeping the appropriate distance between fixtures as determined by the light distribution curves. Either 2 ft by 4 ft (600 by 1200) or 2 ft by 2 ft (600 by 600) fixtures may be used, but they should not be mixed in the same room. Where possible, fixtures should be 1 ft to 3 ft (300 to 900) from the walls, and in no case more than 4 ft (1200).

Step 2 Lay out the compact fluorescent downlights, keeping the appropriate distance between them as determined by the light distribution curves.

Step 3 Lay out the ceiling grid in each room separately using the light fixture locations as a guide. Center the grid to allow for an even distribution of lighting fixtures. The grid may be rotated in either direction.

Step 4 Locate the rigid ductwork, conforming to the requirements stated in the program. The ductwork must be within a specified distance from beams and bearing walls and may run between joists. Rigid ductwork must be planned in an efficient manner.

Step 5 Locate the required number of supply air diffusers using the guidelines stated in the program. Try to locate them so as not to exceed the maximum allowable length of flexible ductwork.

Step 6 Connect the rigid ductwork with the supply air diffusers using flexible ductwork. The flexible ductwork must not be longer than the maximum distance stated in the program, usually 10 ft (3050).

Step 7 Locate the required number of return air grilles. Try to keep the return air grilles on the opposite side of the room from the supply air diffusers, and in no case nearer than 4 ft (1200) from the diffusers.

Step 8 Locate a rigid duct from the plenum to the main return air riser. Locate fire dampers in fire-rated walls using the appropriate symbol.

Step 9 Locate additional programmatic requirements, such as accent lighting and exit signs.

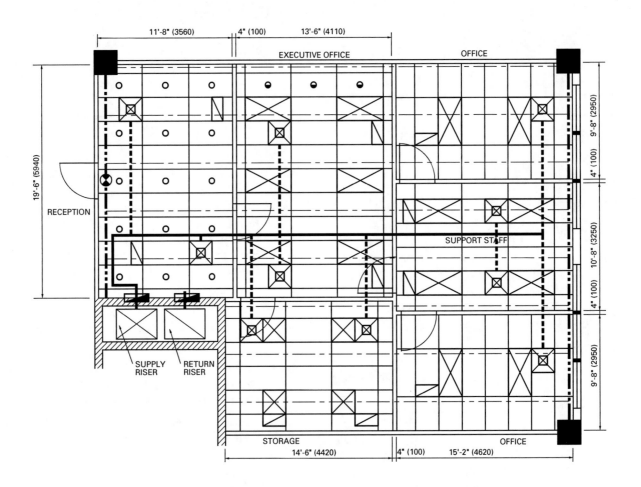

Scale: 1/8" = 1'-0"
[1:100 metric]

**MECHANICAL AND ELECTRICAL PLAN:
PASSING SOLUTION**

MECHANICAL AND ELECTRICAL PLAN: FAILING SOLUTION

Pitfalls

Note 1 The ceiling in the reception area is not laid out symmetrically.

Note 2 The supply air diffusers and return air grilles in the reception area are too close together.

Note 3 The recessed compact fluorescent downlights are spaced too far apart. The lighting diagrams suggest a maximum spacing of 4 ft (1200).

Note 4 The diffusers in the large office area are too close together given the size of the room.

Note 5 Although the lights are spaced appropriately, the space is underlit given the distance from the walls to the lights.

Note 6 In the north office, the lights are too far apart in the east-west direction.

Note 7 In the north office, the lights are too close together in the north-south direction. The lighting diagram suggests a spacing of 4 ft (1200).

Note 8 There is only one diffuser and return air grille in the support staff area. The area of the room is over 150 ft² (14 m²), so two supply and return air registers are required according to the program requirements.

Note 9 The lights in the support staff area are too close together.

Note 10 There is only one return air grille in the storage room.

Note 11 The lights in the storage room are not positioned symmetrically.

Note 12 The rigid ductwork is inefficient, requiring two long runs when one would suffice.

Note 13 There is no rigid duct connecting the plenum with the main return air shaft.

Note 14 Accent light fixtures are not shown.

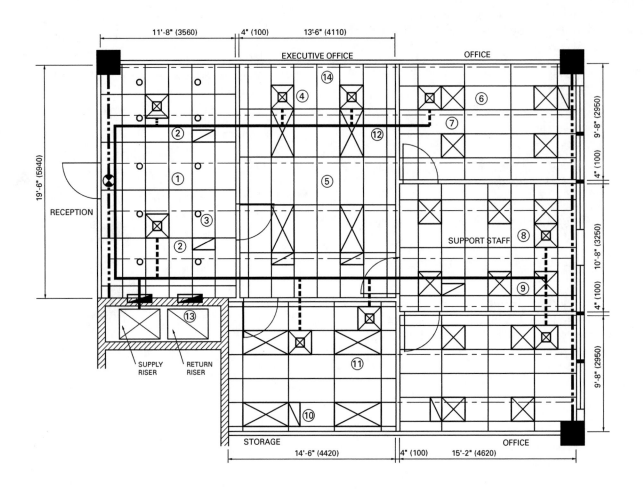

Scale: 1/8" = 1'-0"
[1:100 metric]

**MECHANICAL AND ELECTRICAL PLAN:
FAILING SOLUTION**